CONQUER YOUR COMPUTER

Hot tips and clever shortcuts

Ms Megabyte

Hardie Grant Books

First published in 2003 by
by Hardie Grant Books
85 High Street
Prahran Victoria 3181, Australia
This edition published in 2006
www.hardiegrant.com.au

National Library of Australia Cataloguing-in-Publication Data:

Megabyte, Ms.
Conquer your computer: hot tips and clever shortcuts.
Includes index.
ISBN 1 74066 354 3.
1. Microcomputers - Handbooks, manuals, etc. I. Title.
004.16

Edited by Neil Conning
Cover design by MAU Design
Text design by Polar Design
Typesetting by Kirby Jones and Polar Design
Printed and bound in China by SNP Leefung

All prices are current at the time of printing.

Every effort has been made to incorporate correct information and statistics. The publishers regret any errors and omissions, and invite readers to contribute up-to-date or additional relevant information to Hardie Grant Books.

10 9 8 7 6 5 4 3

Foreword

Just about everyone I know who has taken the time to read, watch, listen to or experience Ms Megabyte wishes that they had discovered her message years before.

We all muddle through knowing that there must be better and faster ways to get jobs done with our computers, but we can't bear the thought of wading through traditional computer manuals, or sitting through a tedious computer class.

There are countless books on computers but the thing that I hear time and time again is that they are all written from a technological point of view, as if the technology is more important than the *person* or the task at hand.

Traditional computer manuals tend to try and tell you *everything* that the computer can do, as if one day you might need to actually use all of these functions. It's no wonder we all nod off at the thought!

Ms Megabyte has an uncanny knack for telling you what you *need* to know to get the most out of your computer. She understands what you want to do with the thing, and she knows just about all it can do. But rather than tell you everything it can do (to her that's a waste of time, and would bore you – and her – to tears!) she tells you about the really useful tricks, tips and shortcuts that turn your computer into your friend rather than the enemy.

Here's *my* tip: For the next ten days spend just ten minutes a day with this book when you are at your computer. You will be amazed at how easy it is to conquer your computer with Ms Megabyte in your corner.

Mr Megabyte

Contents

Introduction

I'm often asked how I came to be Ms Megabyte. The story starts back in the late 80s … I was 21 and looking for work, my strongest skill was my computer expertise. I had learnt everything on the job as a temp and eventually a trainer. I'm very resourceful and love the challenge of being thrown in the deep end, so when I saw a job advertised at Microsoft for a help-desk technician I went for it. It really was the first day of the rest of my life.

As Microsoft Australia's 'tech-lead' for Microsoft Word, I was sent to the USA headquarters for training and eventually relocated to the UK office in 1992. Yes, I met Bill Gates, we all did – he is a fascinating man. We asked him what he did in his spare time and his response, 'I read Quantum Physics manuals', did not surprise.

On my return to Australia I really wanted to settle in Melbourne but the only two opportunities at Microsoft in Melbourne were in Sales and Marketing. I wanted to stay 'technical', so I started my own business doing consulting, training and office automation for businesses using Microsoft products.

One day I was watching an episode of *Healthy Wealthy & Wise* and I realised they had an expert for every area of life – gardening, health, money, cooking – *apart* from technology. At the time I was frustrated with my business as I felt I wasn't able to get my message out to enough people at a time – I wanted everyone to benefit from the techniques I'd learnt to make things easier. That day, I decided that I would be the first TV technology personality.

A year and many, many knock-backs later, I came to the realisation I'd have to start in magazines, so the TV people could see how I got my message across. They didn't want to take a chance, believing that computers could never be explained in an engaging way. Luckily, Paula Joye at *CLEO* saw enough to give me my first break and my first article was published!

Eventually I met Nene King – the 'Queen of Women's Publishing'. I told her about my vision to help the mothers of Australia learn enough about computers to help their kids do their homework, and she decided on the spot that my article would appear in the upcoming 65th birthday edition of *Australian Women's Weekly*. A year later, Nene moved to *Woman's Day* and took me with her, where my column was published weekly for over two years.

From then on in it was much easier to get my message across to the TV producers of shows like the *Midday Show* and *Good Morning Australia*, and for a couple of years I was on both shows regularly, as well as doing various radio segments around Australia. In 1999 the *Today Show* signed me up for a regular Ms Megabyte segment, which ran for over three years.

I also do corporate public speaking, and one of my favourite noises is the 'ohhhah!' that comes from the audience when I demonstrate the shortcut for something they've been doing the long way, such as pressing *Ctrl + Enter* to create a page break in Microsoft Word.

Computers truly are amazing things, they have the ability to extend human potential and are now accessible to everyone. Most libraries will offer free Internet access and lessons for those without computers at home. I have converted many a 'Luddite' by simply finding out about their hobby or favourite subject and showing them how to use the computer to further explore it.

One question I get asked constantly is 'how do you make it so easy to understand?' It's as simple as this: I show people how to get the computer to do *what they want* instead of showing them what the computer can do. You don't need to know all of the computer's capabilities – just the bits that make YOUR life easier!

Anyway, enough – I don't want you to wait any longer to start saving time. Do not attempt to remember all the shortcuts mentioned in this book, try them all, but stick to a few that you think will really help or that you will use regularly. Also, don't be afraid to try something that you've never done before – remember, you can always Ctrl + Z to Undo!

For even *more* hints and tips delivered to your Inbox, join my free electronic newsletter. Visit www.getmega.com, where you can sign up and also find the most current news about the world of Ms Megabyte.

Enjoy!

Ms Megabyte

About this book

When I'm describing something that I want you to click, select or press, like a menu item, button or keyboard key, it will appear in *italics*.

When I'm describing something you should type, it will appear in **bold**.

There are three or four ways to do everything in Windows:

- **Menus along the top**
  Double-click on a menu item to expand the whole menu. (A single click usually displays the most commonly used functions.)
- **Toolbar buttons**
  Hover your mouse over a toolbar button (don't click!) to get a 'tool tip', which describes what the button does.
- **Keyboard shortcuts**
  Keep an eye on the menus, which show keyboard shortcuts where relevant.
- **Shortcut menus**
  Right-click to display a shortcut menu relative to where you clicked.

I'm often asked which method is best. The most efficient computer user knows at least two ways. That way, if your hand is already on the mouse when you need to do something, e.g. **bold**, you can use the mouse to click the *Bold* button on the toolbar. Alternatively, if you're typing on the keyboard and you need to use bold, you'd use the keyboard shortcut to turn bold on and off: *Ctrl + B*.

In lots of cases, the 'long way' will offer you more options for the function you're using, so I'll make sure to show you a few ways to do things in this book.

When I mention the terms 'click', 'double-click' or 'triple-click', I'm referring to the left mouse-button. Where a right mouse-button click is required, I'll refer to it as a 'right-click'.

This is not the type of book that should be read from cover to cover without access to a computer. The parts that relate to the things you do every day will be easy to understand without having to try them out straight away, but I urge you to sit at the computer and try out the other bits, too – you'll be amazed, I promise.

I have assumed that you have been using a computer already and can get by using the Internet, email and doing a bit of word processing.

All of these tips, tricks and prices are current at the time of writing.

This book refers to Microsoft Windows XP and 2003, and Microsoft Office XP and 2003, although most of the shortcuts and tricks will work for any version of Windows and Office.

The shortcuts will often work in the Macintosh version of the program by substituting the *Command* key for *Ctrl*.

Windows

I worked in technical support at Microsoft for many years, and came across some amazing questions over that time. I'm reminded of the guy who called up the helpdesk once to say that his coffee cup holder had broken. I was totally confused, and asked him to explain further. He said 'well, I pressed the little button on the front of the computer, the cup holder popped out – and I put my cup on it, but it broke!' He hadn't used the CD-ROM drive for its normal purpose yet. This is a true story!

Windows is the glue that holds everything else together. We call it a GUI (graphical user interface) environment. It is intuitive – the icons relate to the obvious, in most instances.

My Computer vs Windows Explorer

Your file management can either be done via *My Computer* or *Windows Explorer*.

My Computer is best used for locating files and viewing the contents of your computer or disks, and *Windows Explorer* is best used for file management, that is moving and deleting files and creating folders.

You should already know how to locate *My Computer* by double-clicking the shortcut on the Desktop.

There are two easy ways to access *Windows Explorer*:

- Right-click on the *Start* menu and select *Explore*.
- *Windows key + E*. (A *Windows* key is found on each side of the spacebar and its use is discussed in more detail later – see page 21.)

Creating folders

It is likely that your computer saves all of your new documents in a folder called *My Documents*. You should extend this by creating your own folders within *My Documents* to categorise your work further. Just like a filing cabinet, this process will make it easier to find things later.

- Open *Windows Explorer* using one of the methods learnt on the previous page.
- Click on *My Computer* and select the *My Documents* folder.
- Go to the *File* menu and select *New*, then *Folder*.
- The new folder will be highlighted – type in a name for it, e.g. **Personal**.

You can also create sub-folders within folders.

- Click once on your new *Personal* folder to select it.
- Go to the *File* menu and select *New*, then *Folder*.
- Give a name to this new folder, e.g. **Sport**.

Now you have a folder within *My Documents* called *Personal*, and a folder within *Personal* called *Sport*. Continue the process to create a *Business* folder within *My Documents* and an *Education* folder within *Personal*.

Saving to certain folders

When you are saving new documents, navigate to the correct folder. If you decide at the time of saving that you need another new folder, you can create one on the fly by clicking the *Create New Folder* button in the *Save* dialog box.

Selecting multiple files

You will need to move and delete files regularly, and sometimes you'll want to move or delete many at a time. There are some techniques that make this easier that you'll love – I dare ya!

- To select a block of files at once, click once on the first one, then move your cursor to the last one (don't click yet!) and hold down the *Shift* key, then click it.
- To select files randomly, click once on the first one, then move your cursor to the next one and hold down the *Ctrl* key, then click it, continuing through the list with the *Ctrl* key held down until you've finished selecting files.

Now you can drag them to another folder, drive, or even to the Recycle Bin. If you can't see the folder you want to put them in, cut them by right-clicking on any file in the selection and selecting *Cut* from the shortcut menu. Navigate to the folder you want to put the files into, right-click on it and select *Paste*.

Finding Lost Files

- Right-click on the *Start* button to display the shortcut menu
- Click *Search*.
- Enter your criteria – this can be a part of the filename or alternatively click in the '*a word or phrase in the file*' to type any phrase from the file.

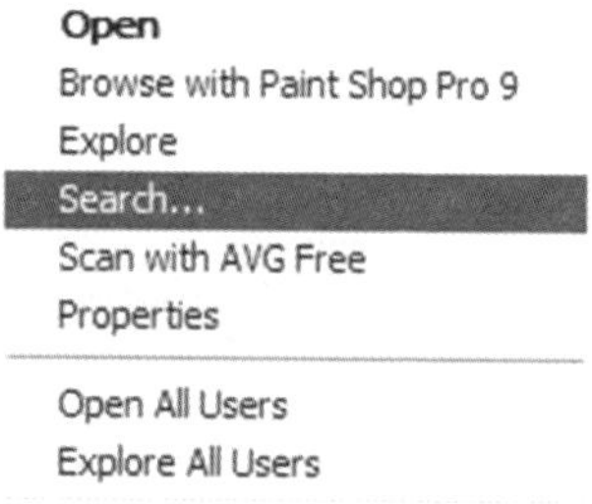

Now check the '*Look in*' setting. Because you commenced your search from the *Start* menu, Windows assumes you're looking for something within the *Start* menu. This is probably not be the case, so we need to tell Windows where to search. Narrowing this down as much as possible will cut down your searching time, so if you know your file is somewhere in, say, the *My Documents* folder, choose that. If you're not sure where it is, choose the *Local Hard Drive (C:)*.

- Click the down arrow at the *'Look in'* box and select the drive and/or folder to search. If you can't see your drive letter or folder, click *Browse* at the very bottom and locate it that way.

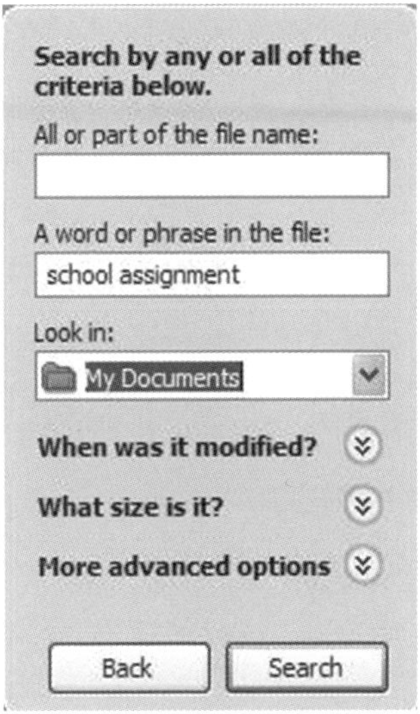

Note You can click on the other options to narrow things down even further if you know roughly when the document was created or what type of file it is.

- Click *Search* to conduct the search.

Once the file has been found, consider moving and perhaps renaming it (see below) so you don't lose it next time.

Renaming files

You can rename any file as long as it is not open. Use Windows Explorer to find the file, then:

- Right-click on the filename to display the shortcut menu.
- Choose *Rename*.

HOT TIP

The keyboard shortcut for renaming is *F2*.

- Type the new name and press *Enter*.

Installing programs

Are you one of those people looking for the *Any* key when your computer tells you to 'press any key to continue'?

Installing most new programs is automatic these days, all that is required is for you to either insert the CD-ROM or click on an *Install* button on the web and follow the instructions. A few tips may help.

From CD

- Insert the CD-ROM in the drive.
- Windows should automatically start the setup program. If this does not happen, double-click on *My Computer*, navigate to the CD-ROM drive, then double-click *Install* or *Setup*.
- Follow the instructions on-screen, selecting the default options when you're not sure.

From the Internet

Occasionally, you'll want to install a program from the Internet. It is usually as simple as following the instructions, but many people get lost at the point where they're asked where to save the file.

- Click the button or link to *Download* or *Install*.

ADSL or cable Internet connection:

- Click *Open* to install the program direct from the Internet.

Dial-up Internet connection:

- Click the *Save* button to download the installation program to your PC to run later.

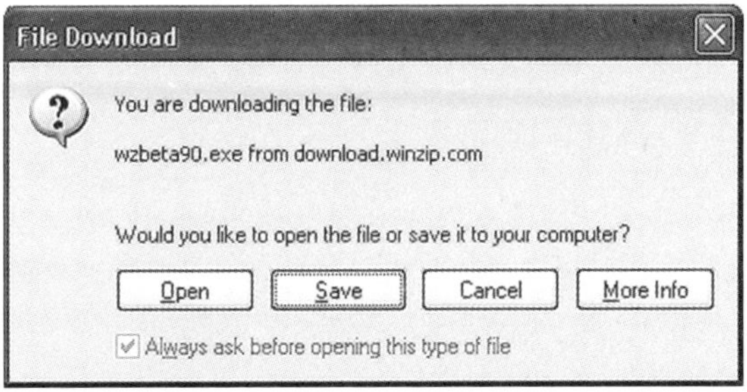

- Either select a file location or create a new one, but take note of where it is you decide to save the file to. I have a folder in My Documents called My Downloads where I save any downloaded programs and files. That way I know exactly where they are when I want to install them or get rid of them.
- When the download is finished, click *Open* to install the program.

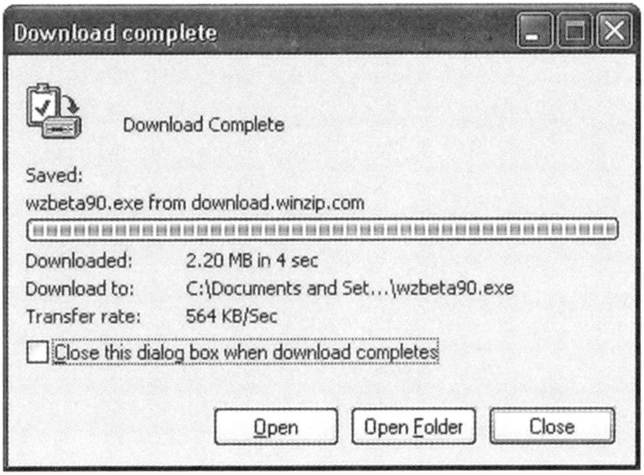

Uninstalling programs

Your PC can get full of junk after a few months, especially if the kids are installing games to try out and only give them one look! Rather than deleting icons from the *Start* menu or deleting entire folders, you should use the Windows Uninstall program, which makes sure hidden files and settings are also removed.

- Go to the *Start* menu and select *Control Panel* (Windows 98: *Start, Settings, Control Panel*).

- Click the *Add or Remove Programs* icon.
- Locate the program you want to get rid of, select it and click *Remove*.

Use *Add or Remove Programs* every three months. Go through the list and get rid of any programs that you know you no longer use.

Renovate! Changing the way Windows looks

Once you've moved into your home away from home (Okay, maybe I'm getting carried away, but I'm talking about your PC), it's time to do some renovating.

Using the Desktop

The Desktop is the screen you see when you first get into Windows. It is just like your real desk – it can be customised to display your most frequently used files or programs, a favourite picture, and give you access to a rubbish bin. It's like a launching pad for everything you need to do on your PC. However, just like your real desk, you should make sure it is not cluttered with unnecessary items, and that it helps you get the job done.

Changing the colours and/or theme

The standard Windows colours are easy on the eye, but if you're an individual, it's the first thing you'll want to change.

- Right-click on the *Desktop* (the first screen you see once Windows has started – with no programs open).
- Select *Properties* from the shortcut menu.
- Select the *Theme* tab and scroll through all the options to find one you like.
- You can also select *Appearance* along the top to have more control over the colours.
- Click *Apply*, then *OK* if you're happy with the results.

Changing the screen saver

Screen savers were important some years ago when the screen could be damaged if left with the same image on it. Monitor technology has evolved and screen savers are simply cosmetic, so have some fun!

- Right-click on the *Desktop*.
- Select *Properties* from the shortcut menu.
- Select *Screen Saver* along the top.
- Click through the different ones, keeping an eye on the Preview window, and when you find one you like, click *Apply*.

- Some screen savers also offer further options like changing the speed or colour of an animation. You will find these options under the *Settings* button.
- Click *OK* to get out of the screen saver settings and back to the Desktop.

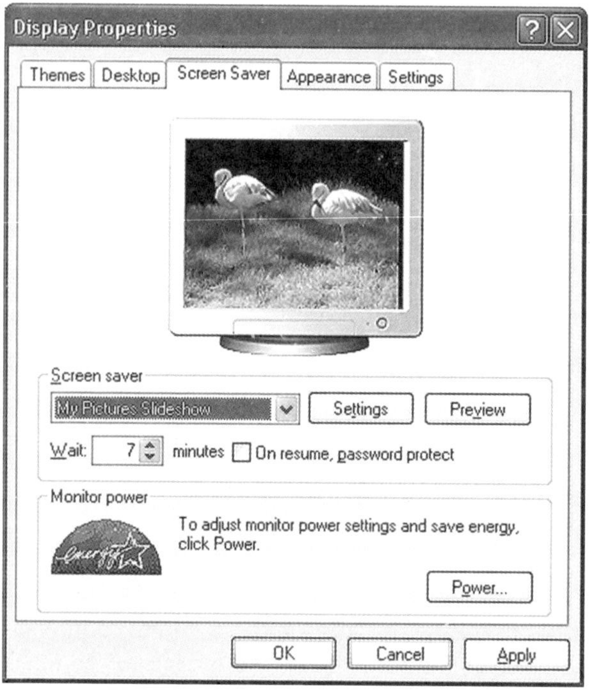

Personalised screen savers

You can choose a screen saver that will scroll through all of the photos in a folder on your PC, turning your computer monitor into a dynamic picture frame.

- From the list of screen savers, choose *My Pictures Slideshow*.
- Click the *Settings* button and click *Browse* to navigate to the folder that contains your photos.

- Click *OK*, then *OK* again.
- Click *Preview* if you want to see how the screen saver looks, or *OK* to finish.

Customising the background

Just like your desk at work, you can jazz up your Desktop to include a personal photo, or an image you find on the Internet that takes your fancy.

To use images stored on your PC:

- Right-click on the *Desktop*.
- Select *Properties* from the shortcut menu.
- Select *Desktop* along the top.
- Scroll through the different backgrounds, or click *Browse* to select an image stored on your hard drive.

For images you find on the Internet:

- Right-click on the image.
- Select *Set as Background*.

- If the image is abnormally stretched or tiled across the screen multiple times, and you want it to appear differently, go back to the *Desktop Properties*, select *Desktop* and change the *Position* setting.

Desktop shortcuts

The icons on the Desktop are mostly shortcuts to the actual programs stored on your hard drive. Your PC comes standard with lots of different Desktop shortcuts, most of which you will not need. You can tell which items are shortcuts, because they have a small arrow in the bottom left corner.

Removing old shortcuts

Remove the icons you never use by either dragging them to the Recycle Bin or selecting them and pressing *Delete* on the keyboard. Remember, deleting a shortcut icon does not delete the actual program. It simply deletes this pointer. To remove the program, follow the instructions in Uninstalling Programs (see page 12) for using the *Add or Remove Programs* function in Windows.

Creating new shortcuts

Create shortcut icons for things you habitually access, such as programs, documents, photos or other graphics.

- Locate the item you are wanting to create a shortcut to. It might already be somewhere on the *Start* menu, or you can use Windows Explorer (remember: *Windows Key + E*) to find it.
- Right-click to display the shortcut menu.
- Choose *Send To*, then *Desktop (create shortcut)*.
- Now go back to your Desktop (the shortcut is *Windows Key + M*) to check you have the new shortcut.

Renaming shortcuts

You can rename any of the shortcuts to suit yourself.

- Right-click on the icon to display the shortcut menu.
- Choose *Rename*.
- Type the new name and press *Enter*.

HOT TIP

The keyboard shortcut for renaming is *F2*.

Rearranging shortcuts

Move the icons around your screen and position them wherever is useful for you. You can set Windows to *Auto Arrange* the icons, so they easily appear in straight lines, but this setting needs to be off if you want to have your way with them! To turn *Auto Arrange* on and off, right-click on the *Desktop* and select *Arrange Icons By*, then *Auto Arrange*.

Backing up

This is one of those lessons that, unfortunately, too many people learn the hard way. Yes, me too! The frequency of your backups depends on how important your files are, but let's assume you have a combination of important personal files, business documents, kids' assignments, family photos and emails. Not something you'd like to lose to the breakdown of a mechanical device like the PC, right?

There are many methods of completing a backup. It really is simply a copy of certain files on your computer. I don't believe it is necessary for the average user to back up the entire system. The files that you create yourself should be enough. I recommend you get into the habit of backing up at the end of every week, or at least every month.

How to choose a backup method

This will largely depend on the amount of data you need to back up. If your *My Documents* folder and your email file weigh in under 650 Mb, you'll be able to simply copy them to a CD using your CD burner.

If your files are over the 650Mb capacity of a single CD, you could opt for a DVD burner – which gives you up to 4.7Gb (most new PCs come with one). This option is also good if you're planning to make your own home movies. A pack of 10 DVD-Rs costs around $15 (which gets you around 30 CD-Rs).

The other option for bigger storage capacity is an external drive which plugs into your computer's USB port. There are many different types and brands to choose from. Here is a sample:

- Iomega Zip drive – 100, 250 or 750Mb capacity ($150-$300).
- Tape backup drive with cartridges ($200+).
- External hard drive – 100–400Gb capacity ($150-$600).

Your best bet is to have a think about the type and amount of data you'd like to back up and visit your local computer retailer to find the right solution.

Backup software

Backup software is used to create one compressed file from the files and folders you'd like to back up. Most good backup software can also be modified to run automatically each week, month, etc.

There is free backup software that comes with Microsoft Windows which can be found if you are using Windows XP Professional:

- Click on the *Start* menu and select *Programs*.
- Click *Accessories*, then *System Tools* and *Backup*.
- Follow the prompts, selecting the folders and files you'd like to back up.
- You will notice that you can't choose a CD burner during this process, so I suggest creating the backup onto your hard drive, then copying that file to the CD.

If you are using Windows XP Home, you'll need to install the backup utility from the original Windows XP CD first.

- Insert your Windows XP CD. The 'Welcome' screen should start automatically, but if not, double-click the *CD* icon in *My Computer*.
- On the Welcome screen, click *Perform Additional Tasks*.
- Click *Browse this CD*.
- Double-click the *ValueAdd* folder, then *Msft* and then *Ntbackup*.
- Double-click *Ntbackup.msi* to install the backup utility.
- Follow the steps above to use the backup utility.

Another backup software that I believe is worth a gander is Dantz Retrospect, available at software retailers.

Finding out your Windows version

If you're not sure what version of Windows you're running, here's how to find out:

- From the *Start* menu, choose *Control Panel.*
- Click *Performance and Maintenance* (if this option is not available, go directly to the next step).
- Double-click the *System* icon.
- Your Windows version information will be displayed.

Recycle Bin

Files that you delete go automatically into the Recycle Bin, in case you want to retrieve them.

Finding deleted files

To retrieve something you've deleted:

- Right-click on the *Recycle Bin* and select *Open*.
- Find the file you wish to retrieve.
- Right-click it and select *Restore*. The file will be restored to its original location.

Permanently deleting a file

To delete a file, you normally right-click on it and select *Delete*, or select it and press *Delete* on the keyboard. This sends it straight to the Recycle Bin. But what if you want to permanently delete it?

- Hold down the *Shift* key before you right-click on the file name, keep it held down while you click *Delete* then let go.

The Recycle Bin will be bypassed, and the file will be permanently deleted – go on, check!

Taking out the trash

Empty the Recycle Bin every couple of months by right-clicking on it and selecting *Empty Recycle Bin*.

Keyboard shortcuts

Windows shortcuts

Keyboard shortcut	**Function**
Alt + Tab	Cycles through all open programs.
Print Screen	Puts a copy of the current screen into the clipboard (a Mr Megabyte favourite!). You need to use *Paste* to make it appear in Word.
Alt + Print Screen	Same as above, but just copies the active window into the clipboard.

That pretty little *Windows* icon on your keyboard (either side of the *Alt* key, which is either side of the spacebar) is not just a tricky attempt at branding by Microsoft; it is actually a useful addition. If you don't have it, your next keyboard probably will.

It offers lots of neat shortcuts for common Windows functions like these:

Keyboard shortcut	**Function**
Windows key on its own	Brings up the *Start* menu.
Windows key + E	Opens *Windows Explorer.*
Windows key + Break	Opens *System Properties.*

Windows key + D	Minimises all windows and goes to the Desktop.
Windows key + M	Same as above.
Windows key + Shift + M	Restores minimised windows.

Rebooting with the three-finger salute!

Reboot is otherwise known as the three-finger salute (as you need to use three fingers for it). Many versions of Windows ago, *Ctrl + Alt + Delete* would restart the computer, but force Windows to crash. We would use it when the program we were working on had stopped responding.

These days, *Ctrl + Alt + Delete* is much more useful and brings up the Task Manager, which lists the programs you currently have running and their status. This way, you can end the programs that are no longer responding and continue working with Windows.

If a program freezes or starts behaving strangely:

- Hold down *Ctrl*, *Alt* and *Delete* all together. When the Task Manager appears you can let go.
- Locate the bratty application by looking for the one that is listed as 'not responding', and click once to select it, then click the *End Task* button.
- Close the Task Manager and return to Windows, where that rogue application should have closed (although it is likely you will lose any unsaved work) and you can start it again.

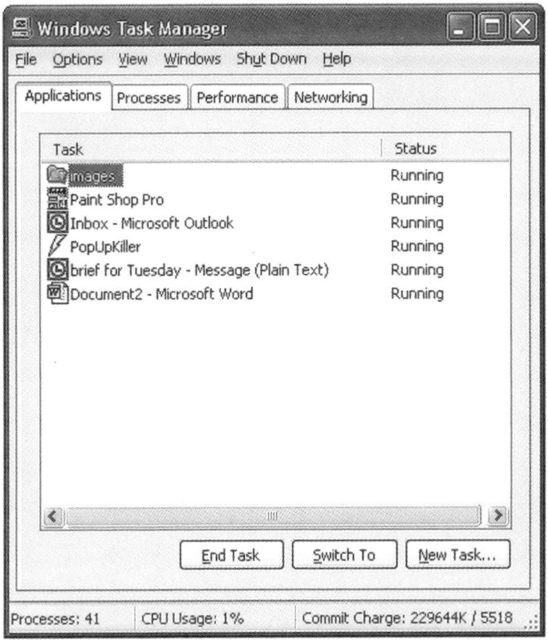

Using Help

Press the *F1* key anywhere in Windows and you'll get the Help window, which can be quite useful if you know how to use it.

- Use the Answer Wizard to type a simple question and press *Enter*. The Help program will scan through your question for keywords that match the Help content and bring up answers that are relevant. Just like the Internet, click on topics to move to them.
- Use the *Index* to type in particular keywords, then double-click to move to these topics.

- Use the *Contents* menu to go through the Help topics in order. Same as above – click on any topic that takes your fancy to move to it.

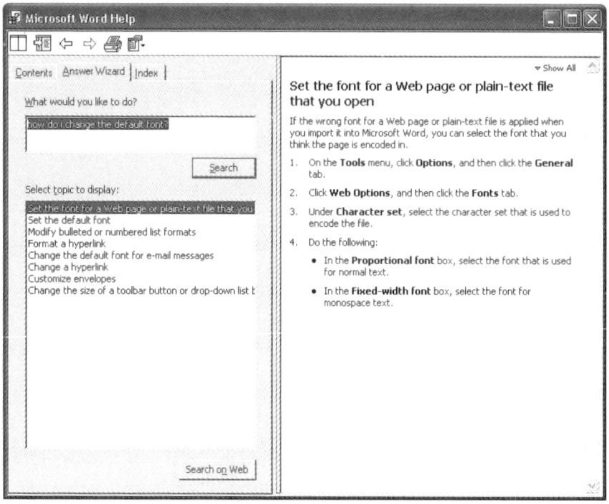

Microsoft Office

Task Pane

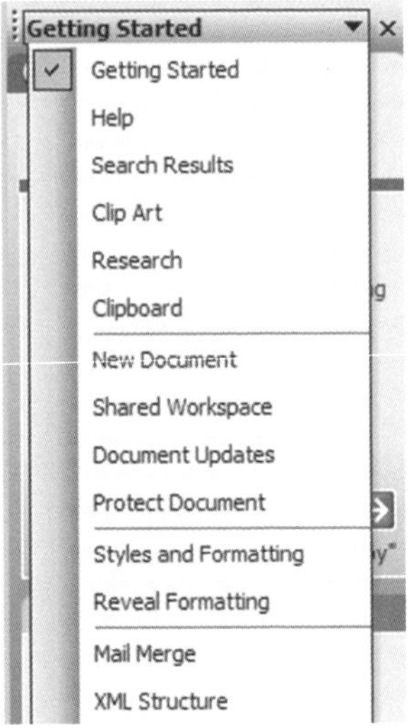

The Task Pane is a new addition to Microsoft Office XP and 2003. You'll notice it popping up along the right side of your screen when you first launch an Office application or create a new file. It's a handy way to access common features such as the ClipArt gallery or Styles and Formatting.

Let me take you through the basics:

- If you don't see the Task Pane, go to the *View* menu and select *Task Pane*.
- The shortcut to open or close the Task Pane is *Ctrl + F1*.
- In the top right corner of the Task Pane, you'll see a *Close* button and a down arrow. The down arrow gives you access to all of the different categories.
- The categories at the top of the list are uniform across all of the Office programs.
- The other categories are specific to the program you're in.

Toolbars

There are many buttons on the toolbars that are common to all Windows programs. Have a look at the first few – New, Open, Save, Permission, Email, Print, Preview, Cut, Copy, Paste, etc.

Some toolbar tricks:

- Right-click on any toolbar to display a list of available toolbars. Click on the one you want to turn on or off.
- Customise the toolbar by right-clicking it and choosing *Customise* from the bottom of the Shortcut menu.

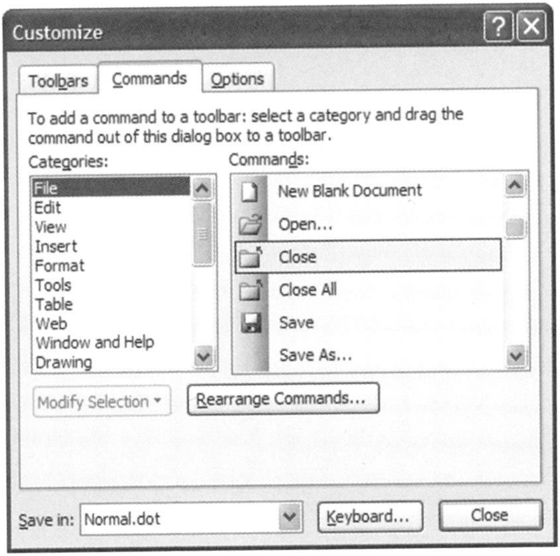

- Click through all the categories on the left, and then the functions on the right of the *Customise* box. When you find a function you'd like to add to the toolbar, just click and drag it up to the location you want.
- To remove a function you don't use from the toolbar, just click and drag it off the toolbar into the *Customise* box.
- You can move toolbars around by clicking and dragging the vertical dots at the beginning of the toolbar.

Images, Graphics and Shapes

For working with photos, see the Photo chapter starting on page 211.

Inserting

There are a few different places to start when you want to work with images, photos, shapes or other graphics:

- The ClipArt library, accessible by:
  a) Going to the *Insert* menu, then *Picture*, then *Clip Art*; or
  b) Clicking the *Insert Clip Art* button on the *Drawing* toolbar.

- The *AutoShapes* button on the *Drawing* toolbar (see Drawing Toolbar section below).
- Capturing the image with a scanner or digital camera, then either:
  a) Going to the *Insert* menu, then *Picture*, then *From File*; or
  b) Clicking the *Insert Picture* button on the *Drawing* toolbar.

- Copying from the Internet by right-clicking on the image and choosing *Copy*, then switching to the program you want and right-clicking where you want the image to go then choosing *Paste*. (You can also choose *Save* when right-clicking if you want to keep the image on your computer for later.)

Note See my section on Copyright in the Internet chapter!

Changing images

Once inserted, you may want to change the size of the image.

- Click once on the image to see the 'resize' handles around it. You'll notice there's one in each corner and one along each edge.

- Click and drag any of these resize handles to change the size of the graphic. Drag toward the middle to make it smaller. Drag away to make it larger.
- Hold the *Shift* key down while dragging to keep the item in proportion.
- To change just one part of the image, such as the colour of the hair in the image shown here, right-click it and choose *Edit Picture* from the shortcut menu. Then click on the part you want to change and use the *Fill Tool* (a paint tin) on the *Drawing* toolbar to select the desired colour or effect.
- To move a selected image, you can use your arrow keys. If you want a smaller, more precise movement, hold down the *Ctrl* key while using the arrow keys. To get the smaller, more precise movement when moving objects with the mouse, hold the *Alt* key down.
- To move a selected object but keep it perfectly on the existing horizontal or vertical axis, hold down the *Shift* key while dragging.
- To wrap text around the graphic, see the end of the Word chapter, page 69.

The Drawing Toolbar

The most common tools on the *Drawing* toolbar are the lines and arrows, and the rectangle and ellipse tools. These next few tips will reshape your frustrations, I'll guarantee it!

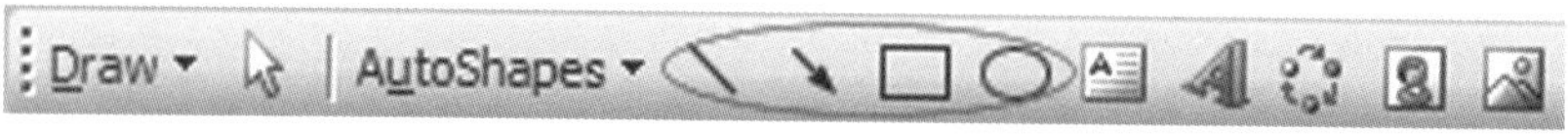

- Click on the tool you need (just click, then let go of the mouse – no dragging please!). As you can see, it is now selected.
- Move your mouse cursor (no clicking yet ...) to the spot where you'd like the line, arrow or shape to start. NOW click and hold down the mouse button, dragging the shape out as large as you like. (OK, let go of the mouse button now!)
- To draw more than one shape without having to re-click the button, double-click it and the tool will stay selected until you click it again or press *Esc*.
- See the AutoShapes tips below for more hints that will work with the line, arrow, rectangle and ellipse tools.

AutoShapes

There are a number of handy pre-set shapes that come with the entire Microsoft Office suite of packages, and you can get to them via the *Drawing* toolbar.

If you've tried to use AutoShapes before, you may have been confused and frustrated by Word's constant use of the Drawing Canvas – a large box that appears with the words 'Create your Drawing Here'. This box is totally unnecessary and if you're bothered by it, let's turn it off:

- From the *Tools* menu, choose *Options*.
- Click the *General* category along the top.

- Down the bottom, click to take the tick out of the *Automatically create drawing canvas when inserting AutoShapes* box.

- Click *OK*.

Now, make sure the *Drawing* toolbar is displayed by right-clicking any existing toolbar and choosing *Drawing* from the shortcut menu.

- Click the *AutoShapes* button and find the shape you want to draw – clicking on it once (remember, don't make the very common mistake of trying to click and drag the shape to your page. Just click on the *Shape* button to select it and then let go).

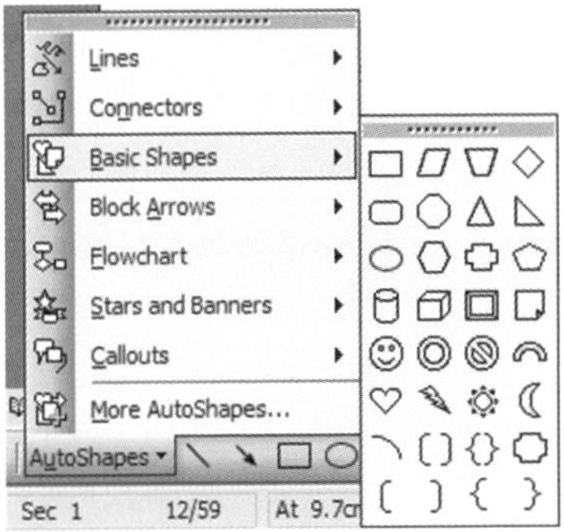

Note If you haven't turned off the Drawing Canvas, Word may create a large box with the words 'Create your drawing here'. Click on the border of that box and press *Delete* on your keyboard to get rid of it.

- Now, move your mouse cursor to the spot on your document where you'd like to draw the AutoShape. (I usually start drawing from the top left corner of where the finished shape will be.)

- Hold your left mouse button down, dragging in the direction in which you wish to draw – usually diagonally to the right.

Some tips:

- Hold down the *Shift* key while drawing if you want a 'perfect shape' ... ie. a perfect circle instead of an oval.
- Hold down the *Ctrl* key while drawing if you wish your object to be drawn from the centre. The point where you begin drawing becomes the centre of the object, rather than one of its corners.
- Yes ... you can use *Shift* AND *Ctrl* to draw a perfect circle from the centre.
- You can add text to an AutoShape by right-clicking the shape and choosing *Add Text* from the shortcut menu.

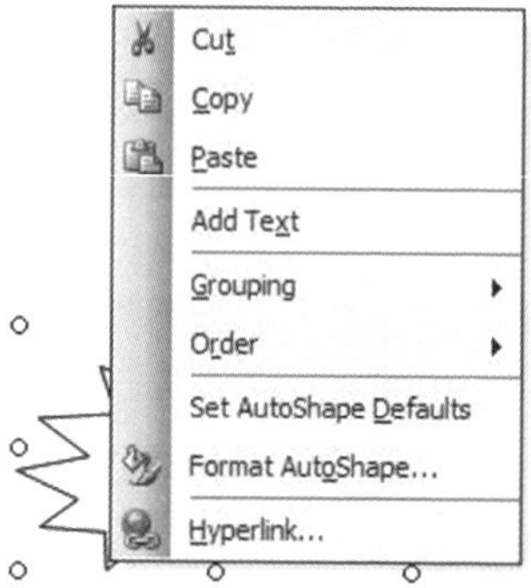

HOT TIP

In Powerpoint, you can click on the border of the shape to select it and just start typing – go on, try it!

- You can rotate AutoShapes that have a round green handle available when the shape is selected. Click and drag the green handle in a circular motion around your shape to rotate it.

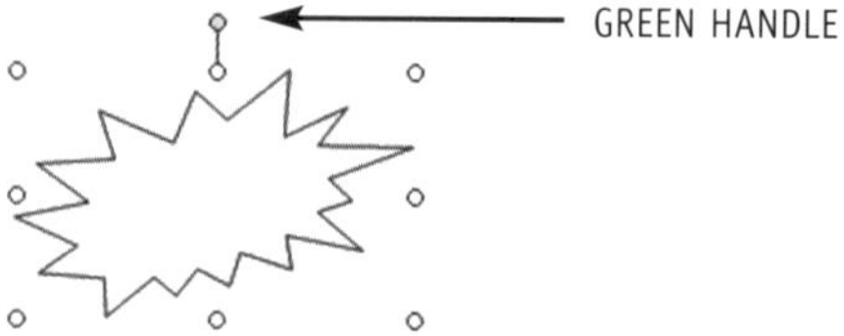

- Float the *Autoshapes* button away from the toolbar to bring it closer to your drawing area – just click *AutoShapes* to bring up the menu, then drag the horizontal dots at the very top. You can even float parts of the *Autoshapes* button, like just the Block Arrows.
- Other handy *Drawing* toolbar buttons:

1. *Fill Colour* – clicking the face of this paint tin will colour any selected shape in the displayed colour. Click the down arrow to choose more colours or effects.
2. *Line Colour* – clicking the face of this paintbrush will colour any selected border or line in the displayed colour. Click the down arrow for more colours.
3. *Font Colour* – clicking the face of this letter *A* will colour any selected text in the displayed colour. Click the down arrow for more colours.
4. *Line Style* – this changes the thickness and pattern of selected borders or lines.
5. *Dash Style* – this changes the selected border or line to different types of dashes
6. *Arrow Style* – this changes the selected line into an arrow head.

Working with multiple images

- *Ctrl* + *D* will duplicate any selected shape(s).
- To copy the formatting from one object to another:
  - Click the first one.
  - Click the *Format Painter* tool on the standard toolbar.

  - Click the second image.

Grouping

- Group objects together so that their juxtaposition remains the same. This is good for when you have lots of objects meticulously lined-up on a page: move one, and you've moved them all.
  - Select multiple objects to be grouped by holding down the *Ctrl* key and selecting them.
  - Right-click on any of the selected objects and from the shortcut menu choose *Grouping,* then *Group*.

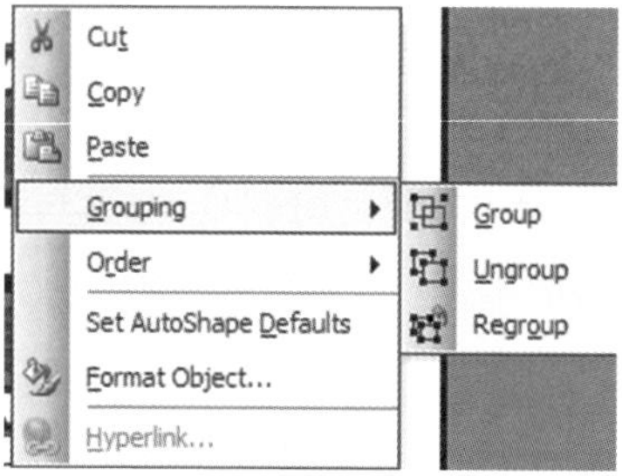

  - To Ungroup, right-click any grouped object and from the shortcut menu, choose *Grouping,* then *Ungroup*.

Layering

- Objects are stacked in layers – each new object becomes the next layer and you often need to reorder things.

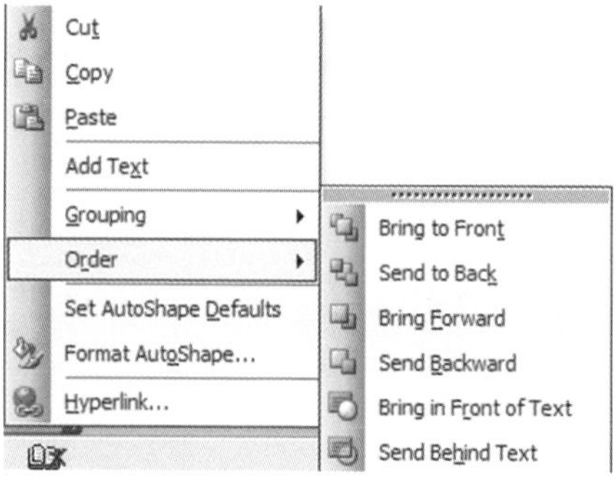

- Right-click an object and choose *Order* from the shortcut menu.
- To move the object one layer at a time, choose either *Bring Forward* or *Send Backward*.
- To move the object to the back of the stack, choose *Send to Back*. To move it to the front, choose *Bring to Front*.

HOT TIP

If you 'lose' an object in a stack, click another object and press *Tab* or *Shift+Tab* to cycle through the objects until it's selected, then use your arrow keys on the keyboard to nudge it out from behind the other object.

Rotating and Flipping

- You can even rotate objects to any degree, and flip them horizontally and vertically – so the Clip Art library really is just a starting point.

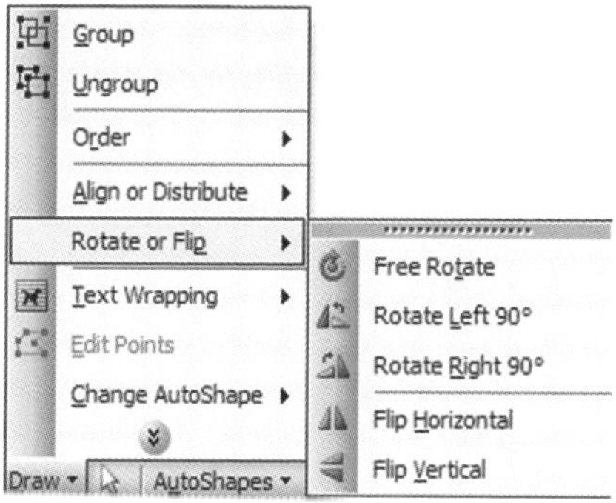

- Select the object to be rotated or flipped.
- From the *Draw* button on the *Drawing* toolbar, choose *Rotate or Flip* and select the option you want.

Creating screen shots

Throughout this book, you'll find diagrams that I've used to illustrate the instructions. These are called 'screen shots' and many people ask me how to do them. They're handy if you're trying to describe an error message to someone who's trying to help you via email or if you're creating your own training guides.

- To grab a shot of the entire screen, press the *Print Screen* key on your keyboard. It doesn't actually DO anything visible, but a copy of the screen is copied into your Clipboard (which you can't see!), ready for pasting into your graphics, word processing or email program.

- Now click where you want the screen shot to appear and from the *Edit* menu, select *Paste* (or use the keyboard shortcut *Ctrl + V*. Or if you're feeling brave, right-click, then choose *Paste* from the shortcut menu).

HOT TIP

If you just want the 'Active Window' instead of the whole screen, hold down the *Alt* key while pressing the *Print Screen* key.

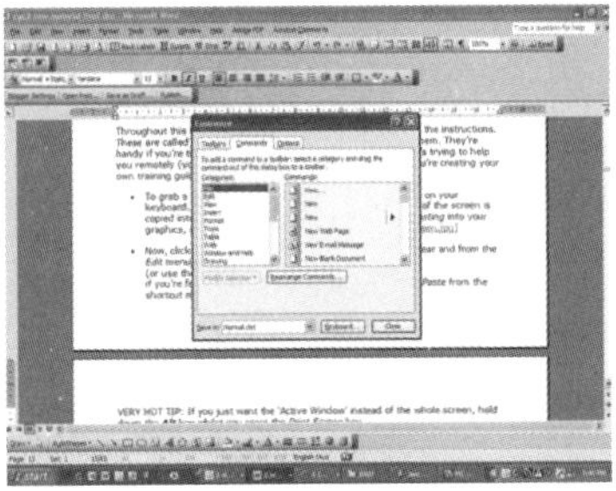

'full screen capture'

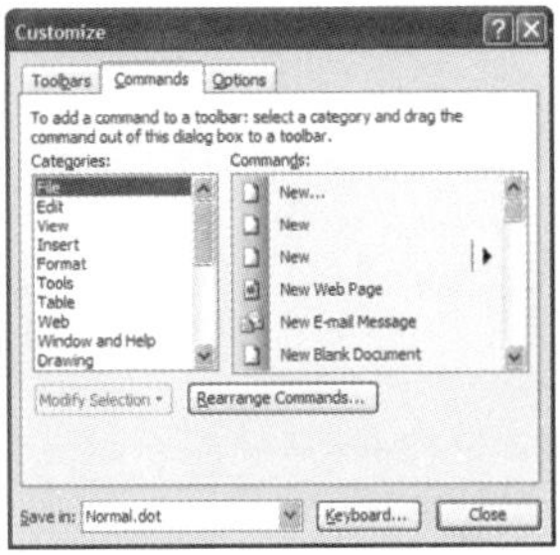

'active window screen capture'

Help yourself!

At **office.microsoft.com** you'll find online training, templates, downloads, help and articles to ensure you really do get the most out of Office. Give it a go – I bet you'll get stuck there for longer than you'd planned!

Microsoft Word

Microsoft Word is used for a large percentage of computer work, but most people are self-taught and find themselves looking over an expert's shoulder, longing for some of their shortcuts and tricks.

Word is a very powerful tool, and many will probably only ever use 20 per cent of its capabilities, but will each be using a different combination of functions to make up that 20 per cent. Some may simply use it to write personal letters, but others may create a multi-page, newspaper-style newsletter or product catalogue with it.

In this section, I show you how to master some of the tricky shortcuts that will give you control of Word, no matter what you use it for.

Out, damn Clippit!

First thing – let's get rid of that damn assistant paper clip, otherwise known as Clippit! The next time you see him, right-click on him and select *Options*. Take the tick out of the *Use Office Assistant* box and click *OK*. Be gone, Clippit! (More handy hints on turning off some other annoying features of Word appear in later tips.)

AutoCorrect – saving time and fixing mistakes!

This is one of my most popular productivity tips for Word, and one of my personal favourites. Think of a common string of text that you type – something like **Ms Megabyte is the Shortcut Queen**. The AutoCorrect feature lets you abbreviate it to something like **gomega**.

Here's how:

1 Go to the *Tools* menu and select *AutoCorrect*.

2 In the *Replace* box, type your abbreviation, e.g. **gomega**.

3 In the *With* box, type the expanded version, e.g. **Ms Megabyte is the Shortcut Queen**.

4 Click *Add*, and then *OK*.

5 Type your abbreviation (**gomega**) into the document and press the spacebar or *Enter* and your text will be expanded.

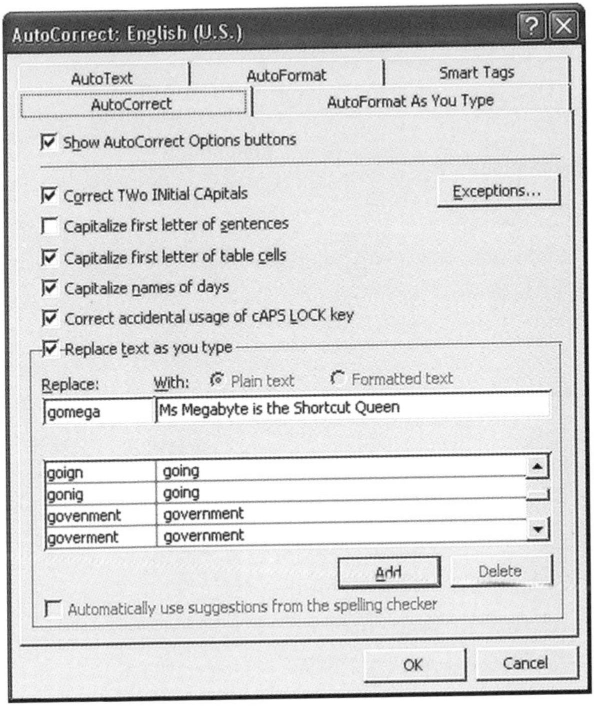

Now you know why Word has been automatically changing certain words, like replacing 'teh' with 'the', 'acheive' with 'achieve'. These entries are already set up and you can browse through them or even delete some of them by going back to the *Tools* menu and selecting *AutoCorrect*. It's not magic after all.

Personally, I had to delete the replacement of 'teh' with 'the' because I have a close friend called Peter Teh!

While you're in the *AutoCorrect* box, take a peek at some of the other options you can control, including the different sections along the top. For example *Correct TWo INitial CApitals* – turn that and other functions off if they annoy you.

Spelling

The spell check doesn't need much explaining – you've probably used it and had no problems at all. Are you using the keyboard shortcut, *F7*, to start it?

Have you seen the red and green wavy underlines all over your document? The red ones signify that Word thinks you've spelt certain words incorrectly and the green ones point to possible errors with your grammar. You can right-click on any red or green wavy underline and Word will give you suggestions on a shortcut menu – simply click the correct one and the change is made dynamically.

You can turn off this automatic check:

- Click to select the *Tools* menu, then *Options*.
- Click the *Spelling* category along the top.
- Click to take the tick out of the *Check spelling as you type* box, and do the same for *Check grammar as you type*.

If you find Word is using a US dictionary and flagging your Aussie words as misspelt, you need to change your default language:

- Click to select the *Tools* menu, then *Language, Set Language*.
- Click *English (Australia)*.
- Click *Default*, then answer *Yes* and click *OK*.

AutoText – abbreviating blocks of text

'Yes, yes' – I can hear you asking all the way from here – 'AutoCorrect may be good for a few words at a time, but what if I want to abbreviate an entire paragraph or more?'

AutoText is your answer, and it's great for standard repeated paragraphs and signature blocks. I once set up a law firm with around 300 AutoText entries as shortcuts to their standard paragraphs.

Here goes:

1. Use your mouse to select the text you want to abbreviate, dragging over all the lines.
2. Give your AutoText entry an abbreviation:
   - Long Way: go to the *Insert* menu and select *AutoText*, then click *AutoText*.
   - Short Way: *Alt + F3*.

3 Type an abbreviation for your AutoText entry, e.g. **sigblock**, and click *Add* (or *OK* if you used the *Alt + F3* shortcut).

Make sure it is three or more letters, or it won't work!

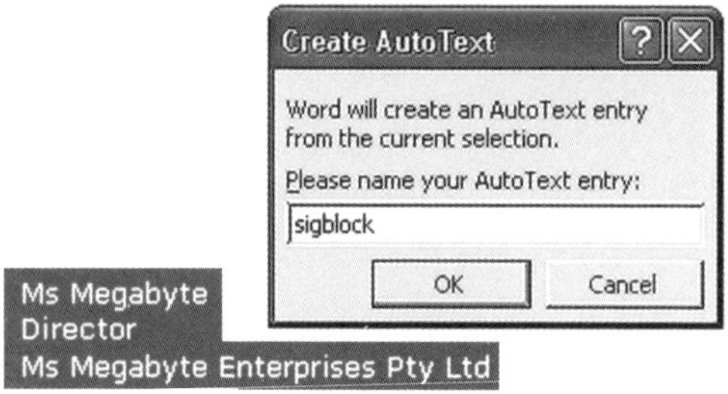

4 Let's test it out. Go to a brand new document (*Ctrl + N*) and type your abbreviation, e.g. **sigblock**. A yellow 'tool tip' box appears, and you simply press *Enter* to expand the text.

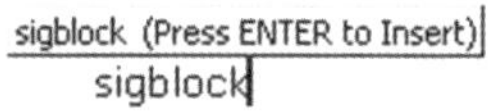

You can print a list of your AutoText entries at any time by going to *File, Print* and selecting *AutoText Entries* from the *Print What* box.

Some text to play with

There's an odd little feature in Word that will put some text on your page. This can be used for laying out a newsletter or testing/demonstrating other functions.

At the start of a blank line anywhere on the page, type the following as it appears:

=rand(5)

Press *Enter* and see what happens – I'll leave it as a surprise! The number in brackets specifies how many paragraphs of text will be entered.

Navigating – moving around better

These are some of the handiest hints around, I promise.

Browsing

Have you been ignoring those symbols at the bottom of the vertical scroll bar over on the right of your screen? Well, they're feeling a bit left out, so it's time to learn what they do.

Let's call the button with the up arrows on it *Browse Previous*, the button with the circle *Browse Object*, and the button with the down arrows *Browse Next*.

- Click the *Browse Object* button.
- Select the last option on the top row – *Browse by Page*.
- You can now use the *Browse Previous* and *Browse Next* buttons to move up or down a page at a time.
- Try it out again, clicking on *Browse Object*, but this time using the other options. You'll find you can browse a document by table, graphic, heading and more.

General navigating techniques

- To move across one word at a time, press the *Ctrl* key in conjunction with the *left* or *right arrow* key.

- To move up or down one paragraph at a time, press the *Ctrl* key in conjunction with the *up* or *down arrow* key.
- To move to the top or bottom of the screen, press *Alt + Ctrl + Page Up* or *Alt + Ctrl + Page Down*.
- To move to the top of the previous page, press *Ctrl + Page Up*.*
- To move to the top of the next page, press *Ctrl + Page Down*.*
- To move to the beginning of a line, press *Home*. To go to the end of a line, press *End*.
- If you press the *F5* key, you can actually choose to go to any page number, line number, bookmark or section.

Finding your spot

There is a nifty feature that comes in handy when editing long Word documents. Especially those documents that you are working on over various different sessions of Word. This book is a great example. I'll finish editing and updating a certain chapter, then save the document, close it and shut the computer down for the night. The next day, I open the document and press *Shift + F5*, which takes me to the last editing location.

Find and Replace

You can use Word's Find feature to quickly locate a particular word, phrase or format in your document. You can even use it to replace all instances of that word, phrase or format with another. First, let's try Find:

- From the *Edit* menu, choose *Find* (Ctrl + F).

*As this shortcut actually refers to the 'browsing' feature, the *Browse Object* button must be on *Browse by Page* for this to work.

- Type the word or phrase you're looking for. If you're looking for any words in a certain format (like Bold), don't enter any text here.
- Click the *More* button to specify further options, like searching for the 'whole word only', etc. Click the *Format* button and specify any formats you're searching for.
- Click *Find Next* to execute the search.

To Find and Replace:

- From the *Edit* menu, choose *Replace (Ctrl + H)*.
- In the *Find What* box, type the word or phrase you want to replace. As before, if you only want to replace a certain format, don't enter any text here
- In the *Replace With* box, type the replacement word or phrase.
- Click the *More* button to specify further options, as above.
- Click *Find Next* to execute the search, then *Replace* to replace each instance.
- Click *Replace All* to replace all instances at once.

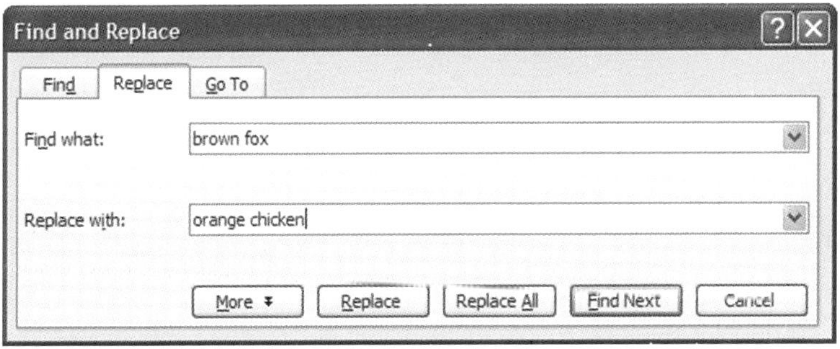

Selecting words, sentences and more

Word is what we call a 'select and do' environment. If you want to apply a format to text you've already typed, you need to select it first by highlighting it. Do this by clicking and dragging the mouse over it – or there are keyboard shortcuts to make life easier.

If you add the *Shift* key to any of the keyboard shortcuts in the navigating tips, you can move and select in the one hit. For example, you learnt on page 45 that *Ctrl* + *arrow* moves across a word at a time. Well, *Ctrl* + *Shift* + *arrow* selects a word at a time. Try it with the other navigating keys.

Here are some easy selecting techniques that you'll never want to be without again:

- Double-click on any word to select the word.
- Triple-click in any paragraph to select the whole paragraph.
- Press *Ctrl* and click in any sentence to select the whole sentence. This is a really nifty one! It selects from the previous full stop to the next full stop automatically.
- Move to the left margin, point your cursor at any line and click once to select the whole line.
- Same as above, but double-click to select the paragraph.
- Same again, but triple-click to select the entire document.
- *Ctrl* + *A* also selects the entire document. This shortcut works in lots of places in Windows – *Ctrl* + *A* in Excel to select an entire worksheet, in your Inbox to select all emails, in Windows Explorer to select all files.

Have you tried to select a large block of text by clicking and dragging your mouse, but been frustrated because the screen scrolls far too quickly?

This next selection shortcut is my favourite – it's perfect for achieving greater control with large selections ... especially when the text spans multiple screens/pages ... I like to call it Point A to Point B selecting:

- Click your mouse once at the beginning of the block you want to select.
- Now, using your scroll bars or the scrolling wheel button on the mouse, scroll down so you can see the end of the block – DON'T CLICK on the page, just SCROLL.
- And the trick? Hold down your *Shift* key and click at the end of the block.
- The text will now be selected from Point A to Point B.

HOT TIP

This last trick will also work in Excel.

Paste Options

Sometimes when pasting something into a Word document, the *Paste Options* icon appears. Clicking this icon allows you to change the format of the newly pasted block:

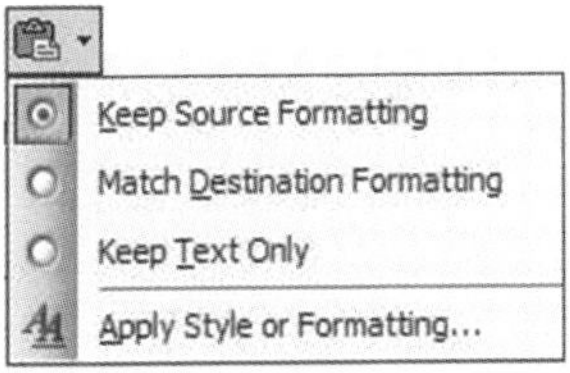

- Choose *Keep Source Formatting* if you want the pasted text to remain as it originally was.

- Choose *Match Destination Formatting* if you want the pasted text to take on the attributes of its destination.
- Choose *Keep Text Only* if you want the text to return to the default format of its destination.
- Choose *Apply Style* or *Formatting* if you'd like to apply a new Style or Format to the pasted text, then select a Style from the list.

Tabs – I know you hate them

I have never understood why so many people hate tabs. Poor old tabs. Tabs were the traditional way to line up columns of text – remember the *Tab* key on old typewriters? The Table feature in Word came along and people couldn't see a use for Tabs anymore, but they are honestly not that difficult if you understand them. In fact, Mr Megabyte was proofreading this text for me and has flatly refused to read this section! Ready for some tab counselling?

There are four types of tabs: left, centre, right and decimal. Let's have a go at creating one of each.

(If your ruler is not showing at the top of the document, go to the *View* menu and select *Ruler* to turn it on.)

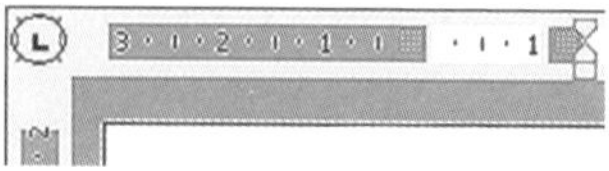

The thing we need to understand is the Tab Selector, to the far left of the ruler. Start clicking on it, go on! Click, click, click – notice what happens? The first four symbols are the only ones you need to know about. They are:

- Left (aligns the text from the left of the tab stop).
- Centre (centres the text at the tab stop).
- Right (aligns the text from the right of the tab stop).
- Decimal (aligns the decimal point in numbers at the tab stop).

Are you still with me? I promise I'll make it worth your while. Give me a T, give me an A, give me a B, give me an S – what do you get? TAAAAABS!

Let's set a few of the different tabs to see how they work. Make sure your ruler is displaying centimetres by going to the *Tools* menu and selecting *Options* from the *General* section along the top, then selecting *Centimetres* as your *Measurements Unit*.

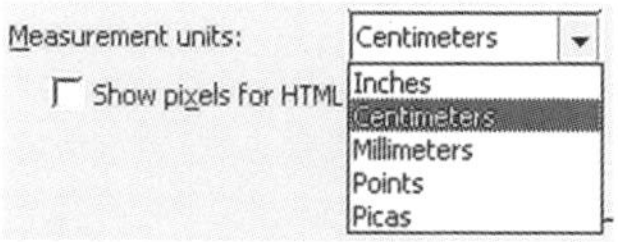

- Go to a new document (*Ctrl* + *N*).
- Click the Tab Selector until the left tab icon is showing.
- Click the ruler at the 2 cm mark. You've set a left tab!
- Go back to the Tab Selector and click it once to get a centre tab.
- Click your mouse along the ruler at 5 cm.
- Go back to the Tab Selector and click it once to get a right tab.
- Click your mouse along the ruler at 9 cm.
- Back we go again to the Tab Selector and click it once to get a decimal tab.
- Click your mouse along the ruler at 11 cm.

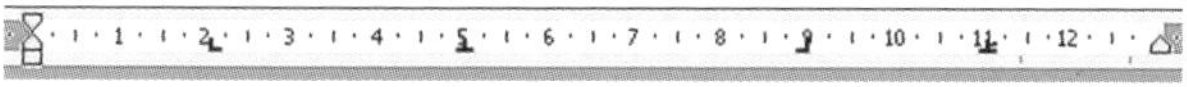

Now you have four different types of tabs set on your ruler. Let's see how they work.

- Press the *Tab* key once to get to the 1st tab stop. Type **bananas**.
- Press the *Tab* key again to get to the 2nd tab stop and type **apples**.
- Press the *Tab* key again to get to the 3rd tab stop and type **oranges**.

- Press the *Tab* key again to get to the last tab stop and type **435.678**.
- Press *Enter* to get to a new line and repeat steps 1–4, using different words and numbers. Watch your text as you type it and see how it behaves in a different way depending on the tab stop you're at. The alignment of the different tabs is illustrated below.

Note If you want to change the position of your tabs and the accompanying text, make sure you select all of the text first. Then you'll find it extremely easy to change the position of the tabs by simply dragging them around on the ruler. To remove a tab stop altogether, use your mouse to drag it off the ruler and down onto your page.

Are you converted?

Vertical selection

Sometimes you may want to select a column of text (a vertical block) that you've typed. For example, say you wanted to select only the bold words in this block of text and change them to italic:

pear	**banana**	apple
kiwi	**mango**	lychee
grape	**melon**	peach

Click just before **banana**. Hold down the *Alt* key and click and drag the mouse down across the words you want to select from the uppermost left corner. Change the format, and voila!

Cut, Copy and Paste

This little trio of handy functions often frustrates new computer users, because there are so many different ways to use them. Five different ways, in fact! You don't have to know all five, but it's a good idea to see what the options are and choose the one or two that suit you. Are you a keyboard queen or do you like button bingo?

To move something, we need to *Cut* it from its original location (which puts it into the Windows Clipboard, the computer's memory) and *Paste* it into the new spot.

To copy something, we need to *Copy* it at its original location (a copy goes into the Windows Clipboard) and *Paste* it into the new spot.

Note If Cut or Copy are greyed out (not available) on the menu, it will mean you don't have any text selected (Word doesn't know what you want it to Cut or Copy!) If Paste is greyed out, you haven't Cut or Copied something (Word doesn't know what to Paste!)

1 The *Edit* menu. You'll find *Cut*, *Copy* and *Paste* up there.

2 The *Standard* toolbar. The scissors for Cut, the 'two documents' picture for Copy and the clipboard for Paste.

3 The keyboard. *Ctrl* + *X* for Cut (think of the X as an open pair of scissors), *Ctrl* + *C* for Copy and *Ctrl* + *V* for Paste (V because it's next to X and C).

4 The right-click. *Cut*, *Copy* and *Paste* appear on the shortcut menu.

5 Drag and drop.
To move: select the text you want to move, then click on it and drag it to the new location. (This is the quickest way to Cut and Paste, because it bypasses the Windows Clipboard).
To copy: select the text you want to move, and hold down the *Ctrl* key while you click and drag it to the new location. Don't let go of *Ctrl* until you've let go of the mouse.

Tear out and keep this handy table:

Using:	***Cut***	***Copy***	***Paste***
Menus	Edit, Cut	Edit, Copy	Edit, Paste
Toolbar buttons			
Keyboard Shortcut	*Ctrl* + *X*	*Ctrl* + *C*	*Ctrl* + *V*
Right Mouse click (RMC)	RMC, Cut	RMC, Copy	RMC, Paste
Drag and drop	Drag	Drag with *Ctrl* key held down the whole time, until you let go of the mouse at the new location.	n/a

Tables – type them out!

Tables are a great way to lay out side-by-side text neatly. They are commonly created by going to the *Table* menu, selecting *Insert* then *Table,* and following the instructions, but the easiest way is to simply type out a few plus and minus signs. What? Yep – you read it correctly – try going into Word and doing this:

+———————+———————+———————+

When you press *Enter,* Word will create a table for you:

Another way to insert a Table (and the method I prefer) is to click and hold down your left mouse button on the *Insert Table* icon, which is found on the *Standard* toolbar. With the left mouse button held down, slowly drag down and across to show Word how many rows and columns you want. When you let go, the table is created.

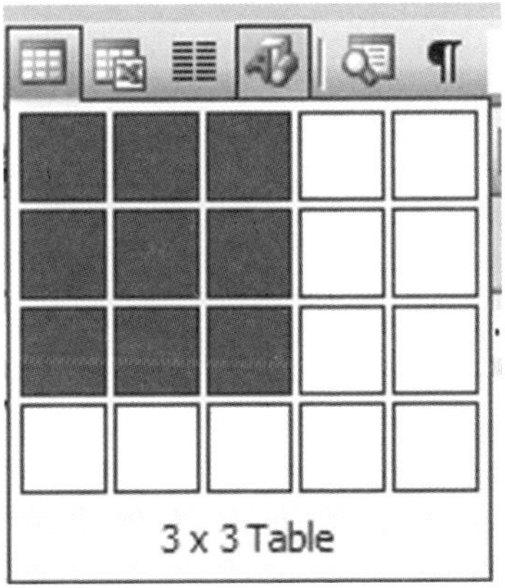

To move around in a table, press *Tab*. To go backwards, press *Shift* + *Tab*. When you get to the last cell in a table, pressing *Tab* will create a new row. I'll create a few new rows in my table:

The *Tables and Borders* toolbar is a smorgasbord of helpful functions, especially the *Draw Table* and *Eraser* buttons.

- Once you've created the table, above, turn the *Tables and Borders* toolbar on by moving your cursor to any existing toolbar and right-clicking, then selecting *Tables and Borders* from the shortcut menu.

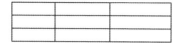

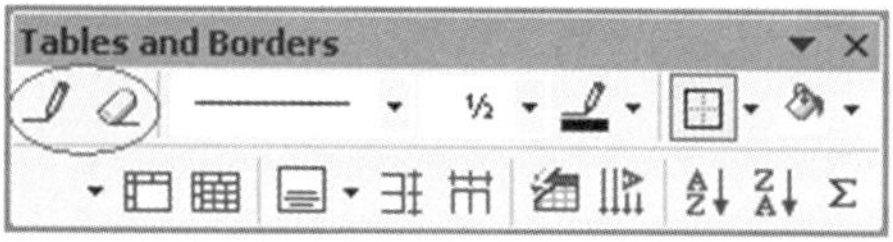

- Click the 1st button in the new toolbar, called *Draw Table*. Now you can click and drag your mouse anywhere in the table to create a new column or row. I'll create a new column break right in the middle of the table.

- On the other hand, if you click the 2nd button on the toolbar, the *Eraser* button, you can click and drag over any existing column or row to delete it. I'll delete the last column break in my table:

Too easy!

Table manners – handy hints

Keyboard shortcut	Function
Alt + click	Selects a column.
Alt + double-click	Selects the entire table.
Alt + Home	Moves to the beginning of a row.
Alt + End	Moves to the end of a row.
Alt + Page Up	Moves to the top of a column.
Alt + Page Down	Moves to the bottom of a column.
Ctrl + Tab	Creates a tab inside a table cell.
Ctrl + up arrow	Moves to previous column.
Ctrl + down arrow	Moves to next column.

Turning table headings sideways

Don't leave the table without this most popular hint. It shows you how to turn your headings sideways. Make sure the *Tables and Borders* toolbar is on, by moving your cursor to any existing toolbar and right-clicking, then selecting *Tables and Borders* from the shortcut menu.

	Sales	Marketing	Finance
2001	12563	2562	32541
2002	25465	3052	45236
2003	15346	2103	4236

- Select your header row by moving to the left of it, outside the table and clicking once.

- Click the *Change Text Direction* button, and keep clicking it until the text goes in the direction you like.

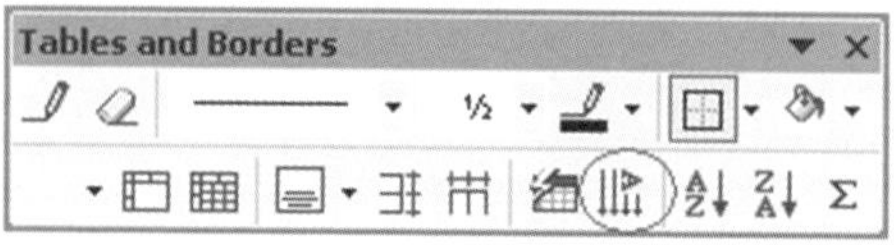

- With the row still selected, click the *Alignment* button to change the horizontal and vertical alignment of the text to your liking.

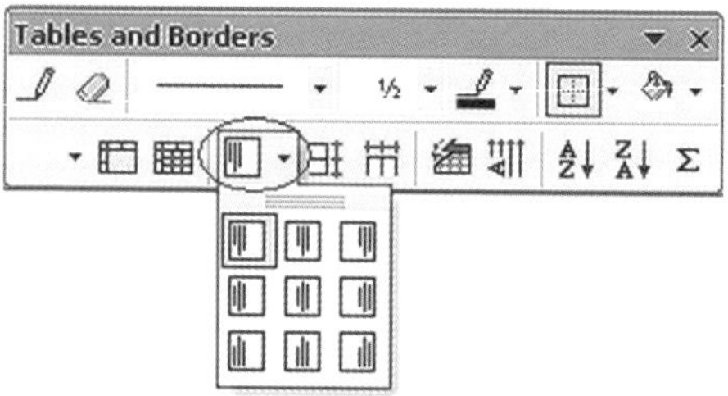

Table gridlines

Turn the table gridlines on whenever you're editing a table. In fact, I never turn them off. If I want to see what my table will look like on a printout, I check *Print Preview* on the *File* menu. To turn gridlines on or off, go to the *Table* menu and select *Show Gridlines*.

AutoFit

You can AutoFit column widths to their widest piece of text by moving your cursor slowly to the column break, waiting for the double-headed arrow to appear and double-clicking. This tip also works for rows.

It is best to have *Table Gridlines* turned on for this tip.

Right-click – it's your friend!

If you've never used the right mouse button, your life is about to change. Go and take a look at yourself in the mirror, because you'll never be the same after this tip. ;-)

The right mouse button brings up what we call a 'context-sensitive menu'. It is a shortcut menu that is relevant to the spot where you clicked. It works almost everywhere in Windows.

Examples of uses for the right mouse button:

Right-click on	**To see**
Toolbars	A selection of toolbars.
Tables	Table options.
Text	Text formatting options.
Pictures	Picture options.

Don't forget – it works in other Windows programs, too. Try it in Excel and your email program.

Customising Word – make it yours

Word comes with a few default settings that are simply annoying. Let's turn them off.

Changing the ruler to Aussie settings

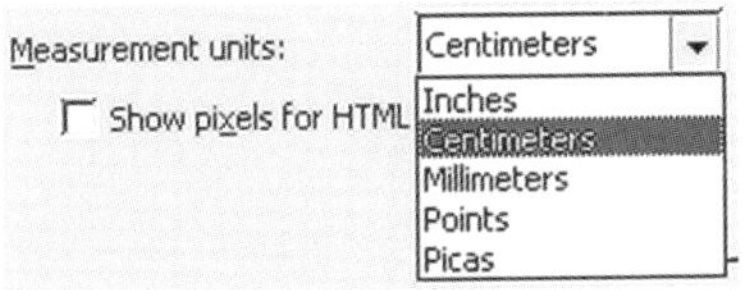

Change your ruler from inches to centimetres by going to the *Tools* menu and selecting *Options*. You'll find the setting in the *General* tab.

Changing the default font to something you like

Change your default font (honestly, who uses Times New Roman 10 anymore?) by going to the *Format* menu and selecting *Font*. Choose the font and size you prefer and click the *Default* button then *OK*. Answer *Yes* when reminded that the change will affect all new documents.

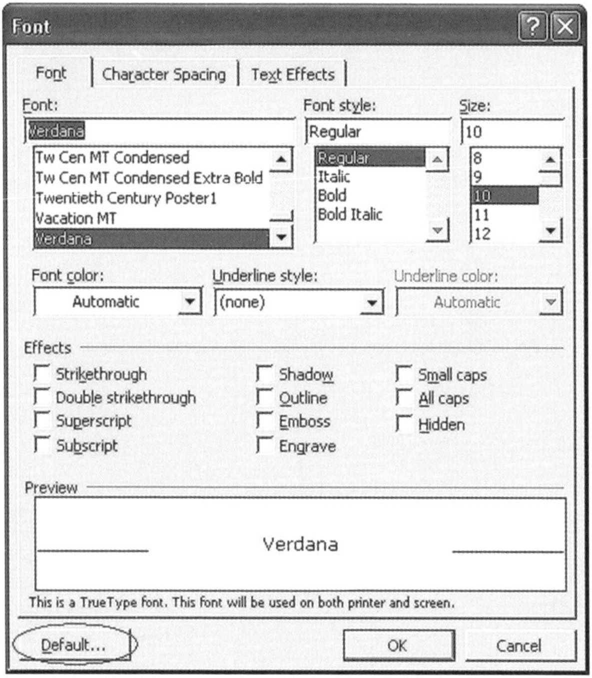

Changing the default file location to something useful

If you are storing your documents somewhere other than the *My Documents* folder, you should change your default file location so Word automatically navigates to that folder when opening or saving files.

1. Go to the *Tools* menu and select *Options*.
2. Click on the *File Locations* tab and select *Documents*.
3. Click *Modify* and locate the folder you want as your default, then double-click it.
4. Click *OK*, then *OK* again.

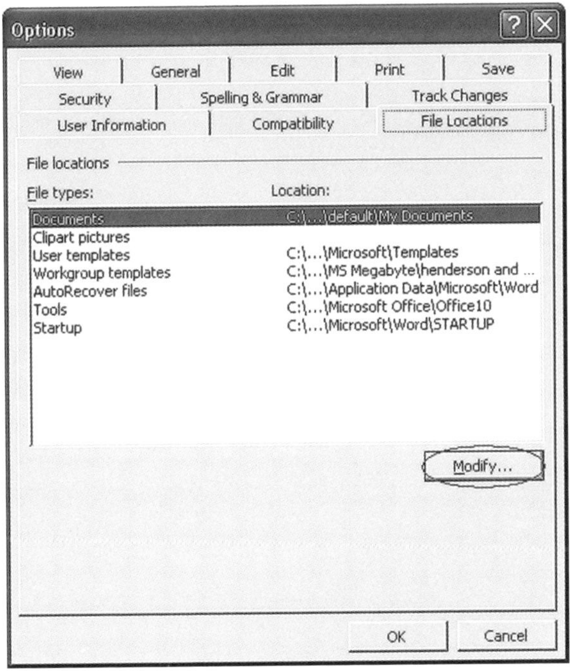

Getting all of your menu functions back

HOT TIP

Have you noticed that Word has a 'clever' way of shortening all of the menus to the most recently used functions? You click on the *View* menu to get to the Header/Footer options, but you have to click the little down arrows at the bottom to expand the menu fully.

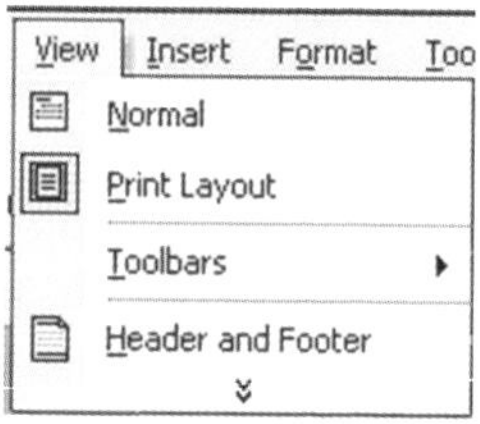

Not anymore! If you double-click at the top of the menu, it will fully expand.

To set Word to show full menus at all times:

- Right-click on any existing toolbar.
- From the shortcut menu, choose *Customise*.
- In the *Options* category, click in the *Always show full menus* box.

Formatting – the cheat sheet

I could write another book on all of the formatting tricks for Word, but you're reading *this* book, so I'll give you the most useful ones.

Using Format Painter

Have you ever wondered what that little paintbrush icon on the toolbar is for? Most people ignore it, but then use it often once they realise what it does. It copies formatting from one piece of text to another. Here's how:

1. Select some text that you'd like to copy the formatting from.
2. Click the *Format Painter* button then move your mouse around the screen without clicking – notice the little paintbrush attached to your cursor?
3. Move the cursor to the beginning of the text that is to receive the formatting and click and drag over it. When you let the mouse button go, the selected text will be formatted in the style of the original text.

Note The Format Painter tool turns off after you've used it once. If you wanted to copy formatting to more than one location, you need to double-click the button at step 2. One at a time, drag over all of the bits of text you'd like to format then press *ESC* when you're finished, to turn the Format Painter off.

Inserting a page break

You can force a page break in Word by holding down the *Ctrl* key and pressing *Enter*. Yes, there are still lots of people who press *Enter* 25 times to make Word create a page break! (Pssst! Pass it on – use *Ctrl* + *Enter* instead!)

Formatting shortcuts you can't be without (well, I can't anyway!)

Ctrl + Shift + >	Increases font size.
Ctrl + Shift + <	Decreases font size.
Ctrl + B	Bold.
Ctrl + I	Italic.
Ctrl + U	Underline.
Ctrl + D	Font dialog box.
Ctrl + Shift + F	Font toolbar box.
Ctrl + Shift + P	Font size toolbar box.
Ctrl + 2	Double line spacing.
Ctrl + 5	1.5 line spacing.
Ctrl + 1	Single line spacing.
Ctrl + 0	Puts an automatic space above the paragraph. This is a good shortcut to pressing *Enter* twice after each paragraph.
Ctrl + Shift + K	Formats Characters as Small Capitals, a Good Alternative to Bold or Underlined Headings.
Ctrl + '='	Subscript formatting, lowering the selected letters $_{\text{below}}$ the regular formatting.
Ctrl + Shift + '='	Superscript formatting, raising the selected letters ^{above} the regular formatting.
Ctrl + Space	Will remove the character formatting from selected text.
Ctrl + Q	Will remove the paragraph formatting from selected text.
Ctrl + L	Left alignment.
Ctrl + R	Right alignment.
Ctrl + J	Justify. This will add space between words to ensure the left and right sides of your paragraph are flush with the left and right margins.
Ctrl + E	Centre alignment.

Ctrl + M	Increases left indent.
Ctrl + Shift + M	Decreases left indent.
Ctrl + T	Hanging indent (for numbered or bulleted lists).
Ctrl + Shift + T	Removes hanging indent.

General keyboard shortcuts – my favourites

Shift + F3	Toggles the case of selected text from UPPER CASE to lower case to Title Case.
Ctrl + F6	Moves from one open Word document to the next.
Ctrl + Z	Undo. My mother-in-law's favourite. (Hello, Dawn!)
F1	Help, which can actually be quite useful, you know.
Ctrl + W	Closes a document.
Alt + F4	Exits Word.
Ctrl + X	Cut.
Ctrl + C	Copy.
Ctrl + V	Paste.
Ctrl + Del	Deletes a word at a time, from the right.
Ctrl + Backspace	Deletes a word at a time, from the left.
Ctrl + A	Selects entire document.
F7	Spell check, but I use it mostly for particular words by double-clicking to select just that word before pressing *F7*.
Shift + F7	Thesaurus. I sometimes use it a word at a time too.
Ctrl + Enter	Forces a page break.
Ctrl + F2	Gets into and out of Print Preview.
Alt + Shift + D	Inserts current date and time. If you don't like the date format that appears, go to the *Start* menu, select *Control Panel* and *Regional Settings* to set a new date format.

Creating your own keyboard shortcuts using Macros

This tip is unbeatable when you find you're stuck in the habit of using the same combination of keystrokes, formatting and text. You can assign that combination to a simple keystroke, saving tons of time!

For example, say you are habitually formatting selected text as Red, Verdana 14, 1.5 line spaced and indented.

- First, select the text to be formatted.
- From the *Tools* menu, choose *Macro*, *Record New Macro*.
- Give your Macro a name and click the *Keyboard* button.

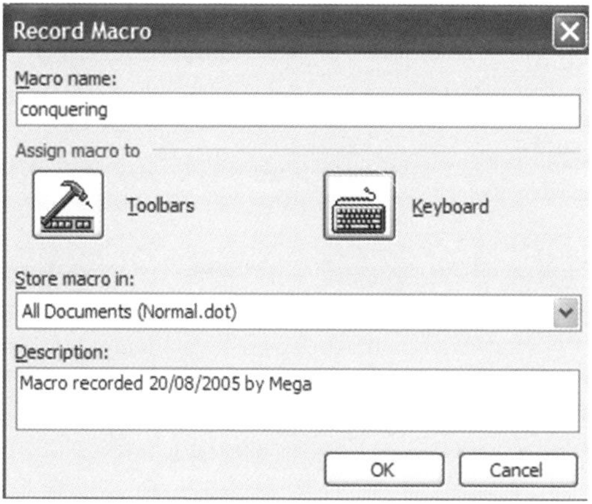

- In the *Customise Keyboard* box, make sure your cursor is in the *Press a new shortcut key* box.

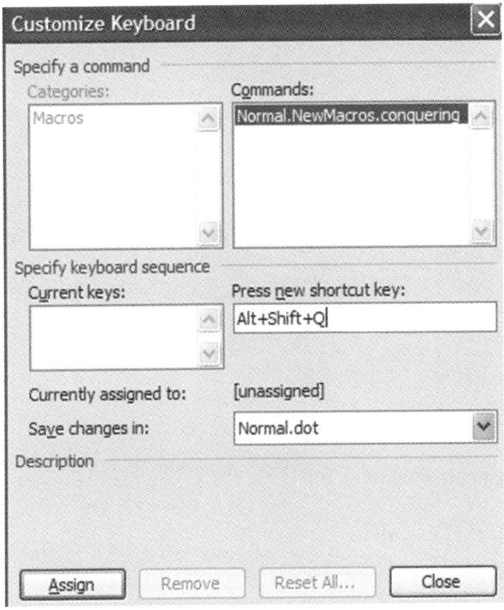

- Press your keyboard combination (eg: *Alt+Shift+Q*).
- Word will let you know if that key combination is assigned to another function. If it is, and you don't use that function often, click to *Reassign* the keystrokes, or backspace to delete them and try another combination.
- Click *Assign* then *Close*.

- You will notice Word has turned on the Macro recorder – you'll see the toolbar.

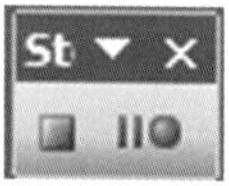

- Go through your combination of keystrokes now, and Word will record everything you do. To follow the example mentioned, you'd do this:
  - Go to the text colour tool and change to *Red*.
  - Go to the *Font* box and choose *Verdana*, then over to the Point size and choose *14*.
  - Change to 1.5 line spacing using the shortcut *Ctrl + 5*.
  - Indent with the shortcut *Ctrl + M*.
- Click the *Close* button on the *Macro* toolbar (the square) when you're finished.
- Now, any time you select a piece of text and use that shortcut key, your macro will run!

Placing graphics into text – jazzing up your documents

Word is so sophisticated these days, that it is only graphic designers who need a separate desktop publishing program.

Using Word, you can create some pretty snazzy newsletters and brochures for your local sporting club, school or even your own small business or website.

To create a newsletter with columns that read like a newspaper article, simply go to the *Format* menu and select *Columns*. Select the number of columns you require and click *OK*. Start typing, and Word will automatically move to the next column when you run out of room on the page. To force a column break, go to the *Insert* menu and select *Break*, then *Column Break* or press *Ctrl + Shift + Enter*.

Whether you're working with columns or not, chances are you'll want to insert a graphic into your document. Not only that, you'll want your text to wrap nicely around the graphic as I've done with Ms Megabyte here, right? Here's how:

1 Insert your graphic. For this example, we'll use some Clipart that comes with Word, but you could use your own photos or something copied from the Internet. To insert Clipart, go to the *Insert* menu and select *Picture*, then *Clipart*. Locate something you like and insert it.

The graphic will appear in line with your text, not as a floating object (your text won't yet flow around it).

2 Right-click on the graphic and select *Format Picture* from the shortcut menu.

The setting is currently on 'in line with text', which means that the graphic is behaving just like any other character – it is taking up its own space on the line wherever you inserted it. We need to tell Word that we want the text to wrap around the graphic, so click on *Tight*. This wraps the text tightly around the graphic's edges.

Now your picture can be dragged around and the text in your document dynamically wraps around it.

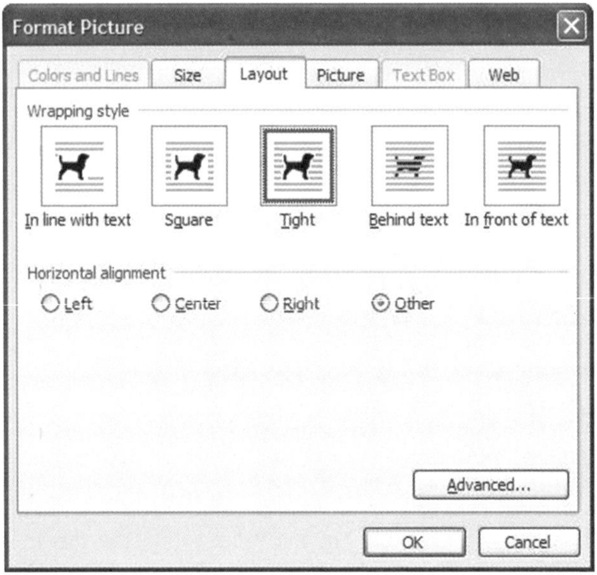

Note In older versions of Word, graphics need to be put into Text Boxes in order to move them around. Click your graphic, then click the *Text Box* button on the *Drawing* toolbar (it looks like a page of text with an *A* in the top left corner).

Resizing graphics

Once you've inserted a graphic or a bit of clipart, it is common to resize it to suit your document. To do this, simply click the graphic once and you'll notice a number of resize handles appear in each corner and along each side.

It's safest to move to one of the resize handles in a corner of the graphic, so you don't risk resizing it out of proportion.

- Start in the top right corner, clicking on the resize handle and holding down the left mouse button.
- Slowly move in towards the centre of the graphic to make it smaller, or in the opposite direction to make it larger.

In most instances, the proportion of the graphic will be fine, but if you notice that you're having trouble keeping the height and width right, hold down the *Shift* key while resizing. This will force the proportions to remain as they are.

HOT TIP

Another one of your computer's little mysteries is how to find those great little symbols you see on other people's documents like ™ ♥ ✂ ©

- Position your cursor where you want to insert a symbol.
- From the *Insert* menu, select *Symbol*.
- Scroll through the available symbols, but change the font to view even more (Wingdings has the best symbols).
- Click on a symbol you like, then click *Insert* to put it into your document.
- Click *Close*.
- If you want to increase the size of the symbol, select it and increase the font size.

For more tips on drawing shapes, see the Autoshapes section in the Office chapter.

Headers/Footers

There is a small amount of space at the top and bottom of each page of your document which is reserved for headers/footers.

Anything you insert in the Header or Footer will appear on every page of your document automatically – this can include text, graphics and even automatic dates and page numbers.

- From the *View* menu, choose *Header and Footer.*
- You are taken into the Header at the top of the page, and the *Header/Footer* toolbar appears.
- Type your Header or insert your graphic.
  - To insert a page number, position your cursor where you want it to appear and click the # on the toolbar.
  - To insert the current date or time, position your cursor where you want it to appear and click the *Calendar or Clock* icon on the toolbar.
- To move to the Footer, click the *Switch between Header and Footer* icon on the toolbar (a white page with yellow rectangles at top and bottom).

Templates

Do you find you're often using *Save As* to save old documents with a new name because the document is formatted perfectly for your needs, and may contain some text that is relevant for the new letter? I know people who work in advertising who've never created a new document from scratch – every proposal starts as an old document. Sound familiar? The danger of doing this is that you may accidentally leave some of the old information in the new document. Like a client name, for example – not good!

Try saving the document as a template instead. Then you can start a brand new document based on that template and simply fill in the blanks.

- Open the old document.
- From the *File* menu, choose *Save As*.
- Give the template a name, such as **Mega business letter**.
- From the *Save File as Type* list at the bottom, select *Document Template*.
- Delete all of the text that is specific to the old document, leaving only the all-purpose text you need.
- *Ctrl* + *W* for Close, and answer *Yes* to save.

To use the new template:

- From the *File* menu, choose *New*.
- The New Document Task Pane appears. Click *On my computer* and a box appears with a list of templates to choose from.
- Double-click your template name and Word creates a new document based on that template.

Mail Merge

Mail merge is the process of combining a list of names and addresses with a standard letter in order to create a batch of personalised letters.

What once seemed such a magical and mysterious feature is now actually very easy to use.

We need two documents – the data document (containing the names and addresses) and the main document (containing all of the text that is common to all recipients).

The Data Document

Your list of names and addresses can be in the form of an Excel spreadsheet, a text file or, more commonly, a table within a Word document.

Creating a data document.

- *Ctrl* + *N* for a new document, if you're not in one already.
- Think about how many fields you'll need in your data document. For example, First Name, Last Name, Address 1, Address 2, Suburb, State, Postcode, Greeting.
- I like to change the orientation of the page to Landscape at this point, so each of the columns has more space:
  - From the *File* menu, choose *Page Setup*.
  - Locate the *Orientation* settings and change to *Landscape*.
  - Click *OK*.
- Now, insert a Table with 8 columns and just a few rows.

HOT TIP

For hints on inserting columns and rows in an existing Table, see page 56.

- In the first row, enter your column headings. See my example below.

FirstName	LastName	Add1	Add2	Suburb	State	PCode	Amount

- Now, start filling out your data document with the names and addresses. In the Amount column, we'll add an amount that relates solely to that person – say we're asking them to pay their outstanding account. Don't worry about the dollar sign, because we'll enter that in the main document.
- If you press *Tab* while in the last column in your row, Word will take you to the first column in the next row. If you're at the end of the Table, *Tab* will create a new row.
- *Ctrl + S* to save and name the document.

The Main Document

- Open an existing document or create a new one, entering all the information that will be common to all recipients. Leave spaces where the name, address and amount will go.
- *Ctrl + S* to save and name the document.
- From the *Tools* menu, select *Letters and Mailings*, then *Mail Merge*.
- Click *Next* at the bottom of the Task Pane to confirm you're creating letters.
- Click *Next* again to confirm you're using the current document.
- Click *Use an existing list* then click *Browse* to select the list of names and addresses. Navigate to the data document and double-click to select it.
- Click *OK* to confirm that you want all records included in the Mail Merge.
- Click *Next* to move to the *Write your letter* stage.
- Click the *More Items* link and a box will appear with the headings from your data document displayed.
- Double-click on *FirstName* and click *Close*.

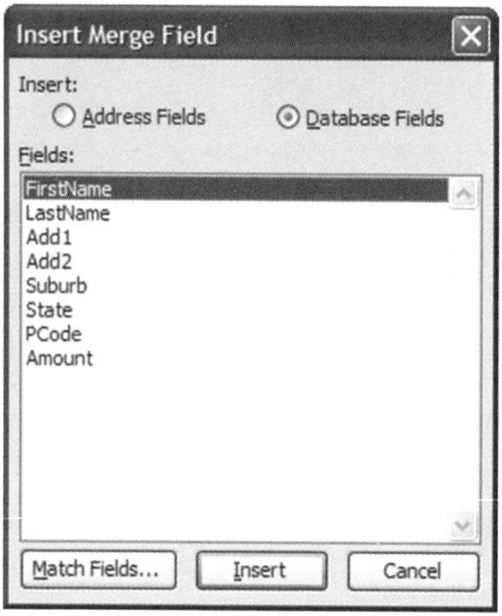

You'll notice that the field appears with chevrons around it as in the diagram.

- Press *Space* to put a space after the FirstName field.

20/08/2005

«FirstName» «LastName»
«Add1»
«Add2»
«Suburb»
«State» «PCode»

Re: Your account

We have pleasure in inviting our valued customers to our next VIP night. Please let us know if you'll be able to make it by dropping us a line via email.

A gentle reminder – your account is currently overdue. Please remit payment of $«Amount» at your earliest convenience.

Yours truly,

- Click *More Items* again and double-click on *LastName*, then click *Close*.
- Press *Enter* to move to the next line.
- Click *More Items* again and double-click on *Add1*, then click *Close*.
- Continue until all of your headings are included and in the right location.
- Click *Next* to preview the letters.
- Click the *Next* button (>>) to preview the next record – notice the information in the main document changing (including the Amount).
- Click *Next* to complete the merge, choosing whether you'd like to send the documents directly to the Printer or *Edit individual letters* to create a new document that contains them all (which you can then print).

Macros

See the section on Creating your own keyboard shortcuts, page 66.

Microsoft Excel

Excel really demonstrates the magic of computing. It is a program that does all the hard work for you as far as number crunching is concerned. The beauty of it is in the simple recalculations Excel will do for you once you've set up a few formulas. And unfortunately, that's where people get stuck. Luckily, there are a few basics that will help.

In Excel, we refer to cells – which are the boxes formed by the intersection of rows and columns.

- Rows are horizontal, going left to right – and are numbered (1, 2, 3 ...). Like Row 4, here:

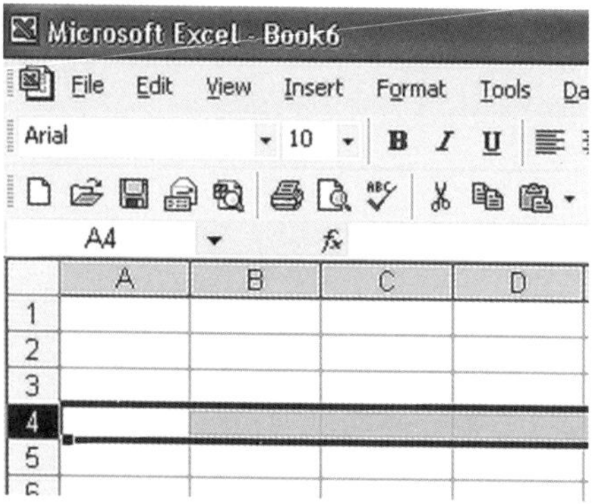

- Columns are vertical, going top to bottom and are alphabetised (A, B, C ...). Like Column C, opposite:

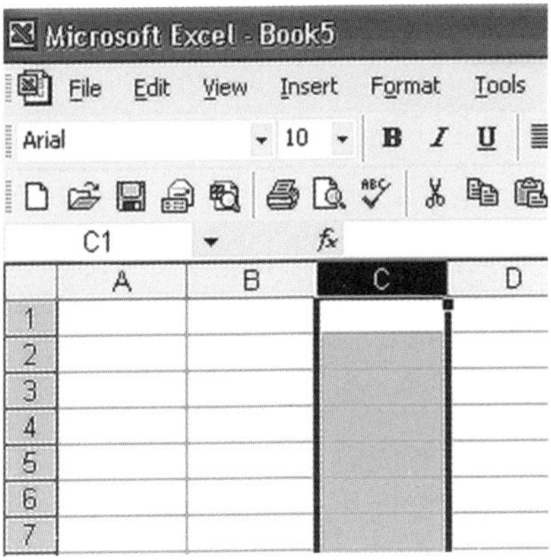

It's like a street directory. In a new Excel sheet, the first cell is A1, a few cells across and down is C3, as I've illustrated here:

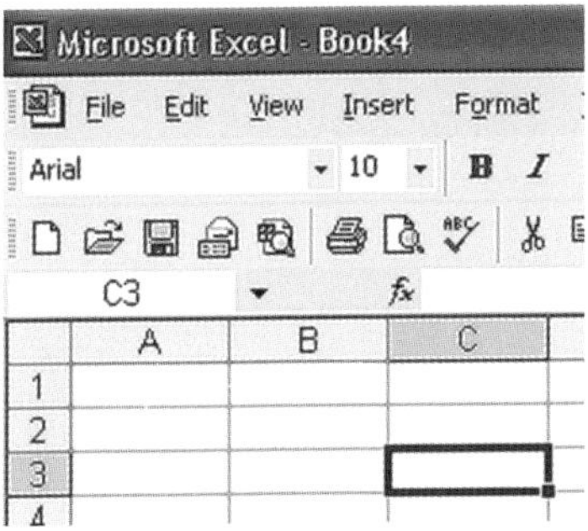

To move around in a spreadsheet, use the *arrow* keys, or the *Tab* key. *Shift* + *Tab* will go backwards. You can also just click anywhere with your mouse.

Formula basics

This is one of those moments when we realise that all that damn algebra at school turned out to be good for something. An Excel formula is usually made up of references to different cells, held together with operators that do all the calculations for us.

Let's worry about the most common operators today, the arithmetic operators that you already know and love, and look at how we use them in Excel.

Operator	**Symbol in Excel**	**Example**
Multiplication	*	=43*8
Division	/	=43/8
Addition	+	=43+8
Subtraction	–	=43–8

Keep in mind that all Excel formulas must begin with an equals sign (=).

- Open up a new Excel sheet and click into any cell.
- We can perform a simple calculation by typing (no spaces required): **=43*8**

When you press *Enter*, Excel will perform the calculation for you (it should come up with 344!)

If you want to edit your formula, or you forgot to put the equals sign in, just double-click on the cell to get back into it. You will also notice you can edit the formula in the 'formula bar' at the top of the screen, as illustrated opposite.

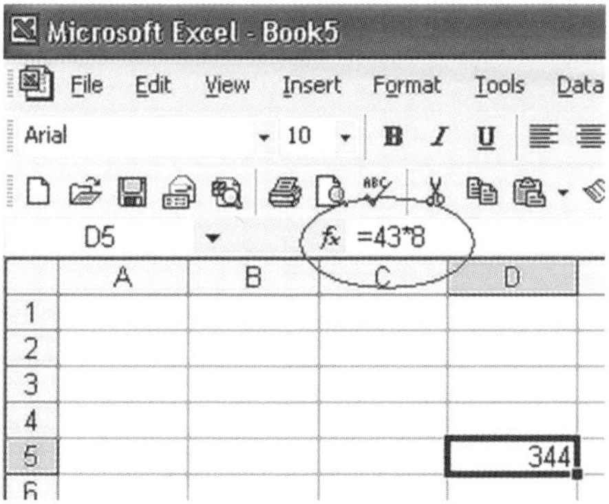

Formula basics plus!

You will probably find that our example above will come up very rarely and you'll actually use Excel more to calculate a value based on the values in other cells, rather than typing in the calculation yourself.

An example is the best way to illustrate this – type the following information into a spreadsheet:

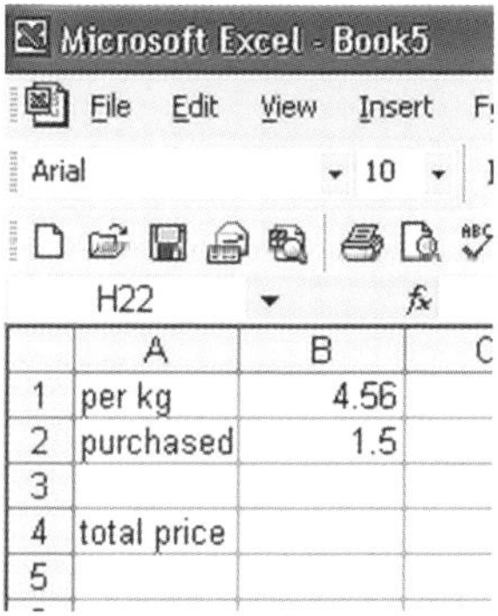

Now, in cell B4, enter the following formula:

=b1*b2

Now press *Enter*.

Excel completes the calculation for you, giving you a total price of 6.84.

Now click on cell B1 and change the value to something else – let's assume the price per kg has changed to 3.5 – and press *Enter*. Excel recalculates for you.

Now you're starting to feel the power of this program – can you imagine how useful it is across a multiple-page budgeting spreadsheet?

Formula next steps

The SUM function is going to be the next thing you'll need in your virtual Excel formula toolkit. It adds all of the numbers in a range of cells. Say you wanted to add all of the cells from A1 to A7. We use the colon character to tell Excel that we want a range of cells. The formula that adds up the values from cell A1 through to A7 looks like this:

=sum(a1:a7)

But the beauty lies in the extra bits you can start to add to the SUM function once you've got a grasp of it. Say we want to add those cells together, then multiply the whole lot by 5:

=sum(a1:a7)*5

Get it? Now let's say we want to add the cells together again, but this time we want to add the value at C7:

=sum(a1:a7,c7)

Automatic cell referencing

Instead of typing cell references yourself, Excel can help out yet again – the only thing required from you is a few mouse clicks.

Start your formula as normal, then click on the actual cell you want in your calculation. Follow this example:

- Type the number **42** into cell B1 and the number **3** into cell B2.
- Type an equals sign (=) into cell B4.
- Click your mouse at cell B1 and you'll notice the cell reference 'B1' will appear automatically at B4. Our formula is gradually being built.
- Type the multiplication symbol (*).
- Click your mouse at cell B2 and press *Enter*. The formula has calculated the value of 42 multiplied by 3, and hopefully come up with 126! Change the values in cells B1 and B2 and watch the total value change automatically.
- To reference a range of cells when you're building a formula, simply drag your mouse over them.

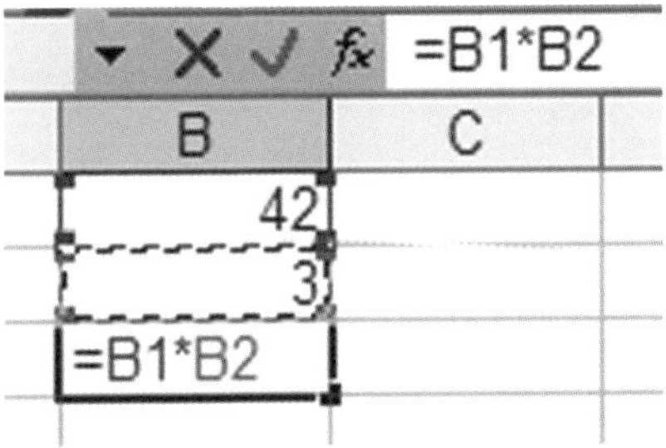

Common formulas

The built-in Excel Help file has some terrific examples of commonly used formulas such as:

- Checking if one number is greater than another.
- Checking the difference between dates or times.
- Converting measurements.

They can be a great starting point to learn more about how formulas work, so check them out when you have time. Either press *F1* or go to *Help, Microsoft Excel Help* and in the Answer Wizard, type **common formulas** and press *Enter*. The list of results should display a topic called 'Examples of commonly used formulas'.

AutoFill

AutoFill is yet another great example of Excel doing all the hard work for you. Excel will take a look at what you've selected, and will then complete the series for you. All you do is drag the AutoFill Handle in the direction you want to extend the series.

Let's take a simple example to start with.

- Type the numbers ***1***, ***2*** and ***3*** in cells A3, B3 and C3 respectively.
- Select all three cells.
- Notice a small black square in the bottom right corner of your selection? That is called the AutoFill Handle.

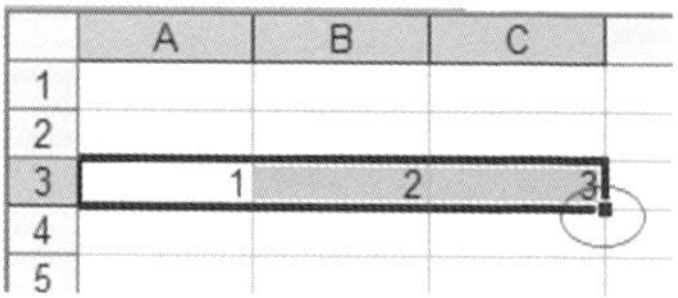

- Move to the AutoFill Handle, and your cursor will change to a crosshatch. Click and hold the mouse button down and drag (slowly!) to the right a few cells. The yellow 'tip' box will give you an indication of how far you've extended the selection. Let go of the mouse button at around 6 or 7.

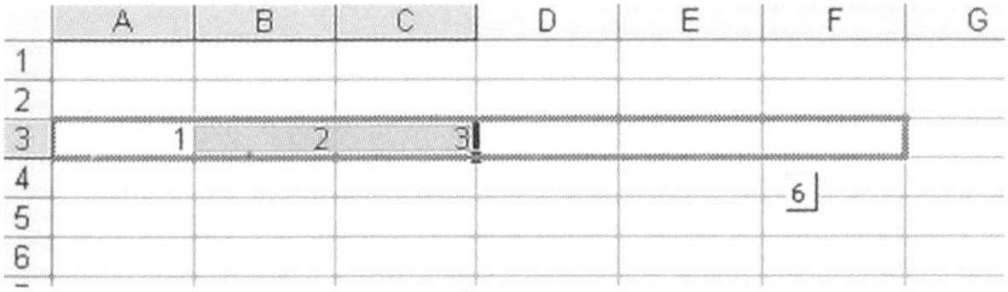

Now try the same thing again, but instead of 1, 2 and 3 – use Mon, Tue and Wed or Jan, Feb, Mar. You can even skip a couple in the series and Excel will continue the same series. For example, if you type 1990, 1993, 1996, select them and use AutoFill, Excel will complete the series three years at a time.

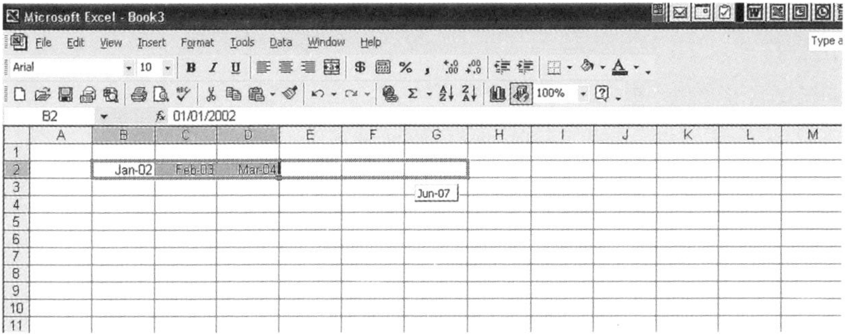

To take things a step further, Excel will even recognise if you've got the same text in a cell, but the numbers are changing. For example, you may have product codes that go like this: PD01, PD02, PD03 – AutoFilling these will give you PD04, PD05, etc. Show Excel the series you're trying to create and AutoFill will complete it for you.

You can use AutoFill for formulas, too. If you've created a formula to add up some figures in a row and the same formula will apply to the cells beneath, simply AutoFill it down.

Formula range

HOT TIP

You can enter the same formula into a range of cells by selecting the range first, typing the formula, and then pressing *Ctrl + Enter*.

AutoSum

How much more automatic can things get? Well this is it – AutoSum: the automatic formula creator. You may wonder why I didn't tell you before I taught you how to build a formula yourself, but I really believe the core to understanding Excel is to be able to decipher a formula, so trust me!

Clicking the *AutoSum* toolbar button below or to the right of a group of numbers will tell Excel to create an automatic sum formula with the numbers. Let's try an example:

1 Type out the figures in the illustration.

HOT TIP

Always leave a blank row below your dates – this stops Excel getting confused and including them in automatic calculations. If you don't like the blank row, include an apostrophe as the first character in your date cells – this will force Excel to see them as text instead of numbers.

Ie. instead of **1999**, enter **'1999**. Excel will not display or print the apostrophe.

2 Click at cell B6.

	A	B	C	D	E	F
1		1999	2000	2001	2002	2003
2						
3	Sales	456	542	213	544	213
4	Marketing	232	221	265	621	315
5	Admin	356	523	123	236	542
6						
7						

3 Click the *AutoSum* toolbar button. (It's a Greek Epsilon symbol – looks like a funky E.)

4 The suggested formula appears, i.e. =(B3:B5). Click the *AutoSum* button again to accept it.

Note You could double-click the *AutoSum* button at step 3, if you're confident the formula will be right. The answer will appear without a look at the formula.

5 Now use the *AutoFill Handle* to fill the formula across to the other columns.

B6 =SUM(B3:B5)

	A	B	C	D	E	F	G
1		1999	2000	2001	2002	2003	
2							
3	Sales	456	542	213	544	213	
4	Marketing	232	221	265	621	315	
5	Admin	356	523	123	236	542	
6		1044	1286	601	1401	1070	
7							
8							

6 Add a total column at Column G and practise the AutoSum feature at G3 to determine the sum of the 'Sales' figures, then AutoFill that down.

AutoSum tips

You can select cells and perform a quick calculation on them without creating a formula.

Say, for example, we want to find the minimum value in all of our figures above:

- Select B3:F5 (B3 through to F5).
- Look down at the very bottom of the screen at the status bar and right-click on the function. (It should read Min =)

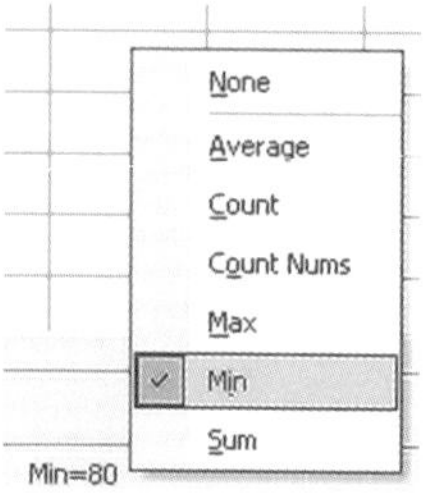

- From the shortcut menu, select the function you want to use to calculate with. In our example, we'll select *Min*. The answer appears in the status bar.
- Right-click again and try a different function, such as *Average*. The average from all the figures will appear.

You can AutoSum more than one row or column at a time rather than do it once and use *AutoFill*. Simply select the cells to be AutoSummed, then click the *AutoSum* button once.

HOT TIP

Alt + equals (=) is the shortcut for AutoSum.

AutoFit

You can resize columns to automatically fit the widest piece of text within the column.

Move your mouse to the junction between the columns and double-click to AutoFit.

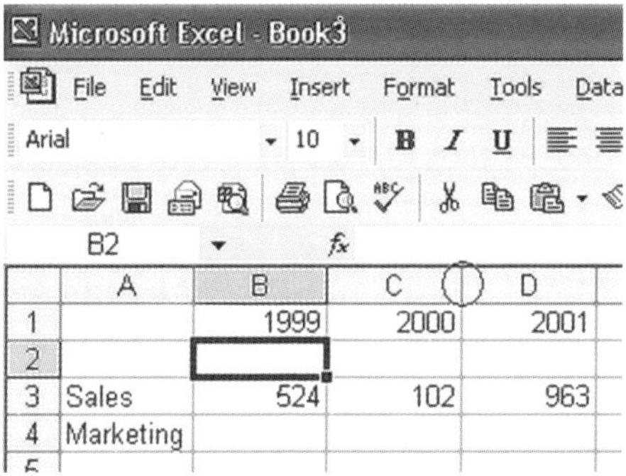

You can select a range of columns and AutoFit en masse by double-clicking any column junction in the selection.

This also works with rows, but is not as commonly used.

Data entry

When you need to enter a block of data quickly, there is an easy way:

- Click and drag to select all the cells that are to contain the data.
- Now, type the first entry. Pressing *Enter* will take you one cell down. (Pressing *Shift* + *Enter* will take you one cell up.)

- Continue this, and when you get to the last cell, pressing *Enter* will take you directly to the top cell in the next column.
- Alternatively, you could press the *Tab* key between each entry, which will move you one cell to the right. Pressing *Tab* while in the last cell takes you to the first cell in the next row. (Pressing *Shift* + *Tab* will take you one cell to the left.)

Range naming

This is invaluable for large spreadsheets, especially when you find you need to select the same block of cells on a regular basis. You can give those blocks of cells names which make them easier to locate and most importantly, easier to select.

- Select any block of cells you'd like to name. (For selection tips, skip forward a few pages.)
- Click in the *Name* box (as circled below) – it will display the name of the first cell in your selection. Alternatively, use the keyboard shortcut: *Ctrl* + *F3*.
- Type a name for your range of cells, e.g. **budget**.

Now, when you'd like to get back to those figures quickly, you can do so either by clicking the *down arrow* to the right of the *Name* box and selecting your *Range Name*, or by pressing the *F5* key on the keyboard and selecting the range name from there, then clicking *OK*.

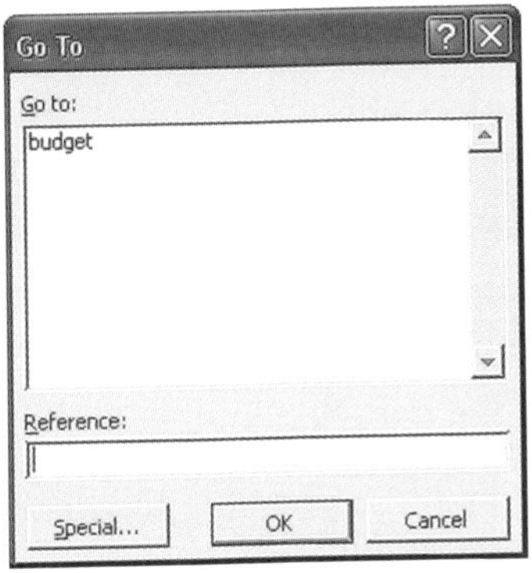

Sheet naming

While we're on the subject of naming things, it can be handy to name your sheets if you use multiple worksheets in the one Excel file (workbook). Just double-click the *Sheet* tab (Sheet1, Sheet2, etc.) and type in a new name. You can change the order of your sheets by clicking and dragging the sheet name to its new location.

HOT TIP

You can even colour code the sheet names – right-click on any sheet name and select *Tab Colour*.

Navigating

Moving around in Excel certainly is easier with a few tricks up your sleeve.

Getting where you want to go

As mentioned earlier when explaining range naming, the *F5* key brings up the *Go To* box in Excel, which not only allows you to go to previously named ranges, but any cell reference or range you like. Let's try it.

- Press *F5*.
- Type **A12:Q54** and press *Enter*. (You don't need to type the cell references in capitals.)

Excel selects that range for you.

Navigating shortcuts

Shortcut keys	**To move**
Tab	Right one cell.
Shift + Tab	Left one cell.
Arrow keys	One cell in that direction.
Ctrl + arrow keys	To the last bit of data in that direction.
Home	To the beginning of the row.
Ctrl + Home	To the top left of the worksheet.
Ctrl + End	To the last cell containing data.
Page Up or Page Down	One screen up or down.
Alt + Page Up or Page Down	One screen left or right.
Ctrl + Page Up or Down	One sheet up or down.

Selecting

A few tips will make all the difference.

Extending the selection

In the previous section, you learnt a few navigation techniques. Well, you can combine any of those keyboard shortcuts with the *Shift* key to select as you go.

For example:

Pressing the *right arrow* key moves you across a cell at a time.

Holding down the *Shift* key and pressing the *right arrow* key selects a cell at a time to the right.

From point A to point B

How many times have you started to select something in a spreadsheet, but as you've moved close to the edge of the screen, it just takes off and goes way too fast for you to complete your selection? It is one of the most frustrating things for self-taught Excel users. Well, not for much longer!

Open a spreadsheet that has a few screens' worth of information in it that we can play with. If you don't have one already prepared, just pretend!

Let's assume we want to select from a point on the screen that we can see, let's say B3 (we'll call it point A), to a point that is actually hidden from view – across to the right or down, let's say R24 (we'll call it point B). Here's how to do it without that frustration of the screen running away from you.

- Click at point A (B3).
- Use your scroll bars to move to point B (R24), without clicking the mouse on the spreadsheet at all. (That is the critical part – no mouse-clicking on the spreadsheet, just scrolling!)

- When you can see point B (R24) on the screen, hold down the *Shift* key on the keyboard and then click there.

Excel will have selected from point A to point B.

Selection shortcuts

Shortcut keys	To
Ctrl + spacebar	Select a whole column.
Shift + spacebar	Select a whole row.
Ctrl + A	Select the whole sheet.
*Ctrl + * (numeric keypad) or Ctrl + Shift + 8.*	Select all cells around the current cell
Shift + arrow keys	Extend the selection in the direction of the arrow.
Ctrl + click	Randomly select cells, columns and rows

Formatting

A complex Excel spreadsheet can be difficult to read at the best of times, but some snazzy formatting can make the job easier, no matter how detailed the numbers are.

AutoFormat

We seem to become quite annoyed at the control that many Office programs have over our choices, but this particular function can be very helpful – if not for formatting our entire sheet for us, at least as a great starting point to work from.

- Click in the middle of a spreadsheet you wish to format.
- Go to the *Format* menu and select *AutoFormat*.
- Scroll through the available options and click one you like, then click *OK*.

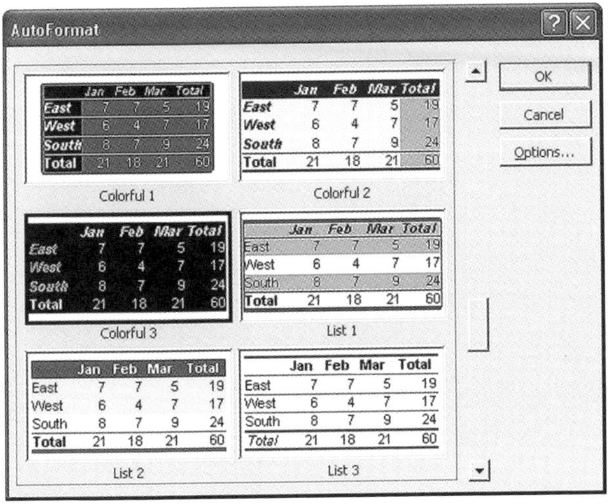

If you don't like what you see, press *Ctrl* + *Z* to undo.

Formatting shortcuts

Shortcut keys	**To**
Ctrl + 1	Display *Format Cells* dialog box.
Ctrl + Shift + ~	Select general number format.
Ctrl + Shift + $	Select currency format with two decimal places (negatives in parenthesis).
Ctrl + Shift + %	Select percentage format with no decimal places.
Ctrl + Shift + #	Select date format with the day, month, and year.
Ctrl + Shift + @	Select time format with the hour and minute, and a.m. or p.m.
Ctrl + Shift + !	Select number format with two decimal places, thousands separator (negatives appear with minus sign).
Ctrl + Shift + &	Apply an outline border.

Aligning text vertically or diagonally

Headings often look great in Excel if they are turned around on an angle.

- Select the headings you want to change, or click on the row number if you want all headings in a particular row.
- Right-click on your selection and select *Format Cells*.
- Along the top, select *Alignment*.
- Select your *Orientation*. I recommend 45 degrees – it looks best!
- Click *OK*.

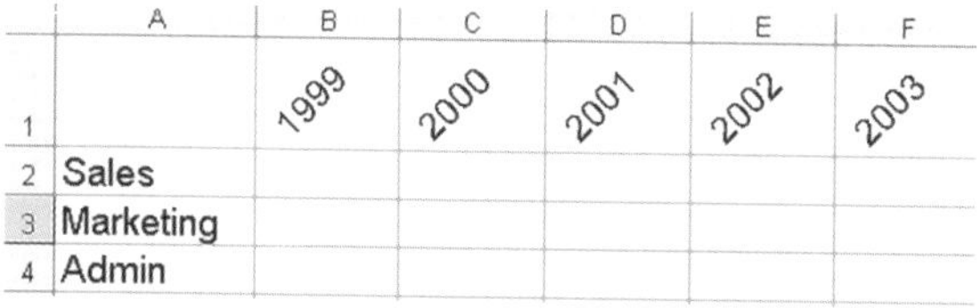

	A	B	C	D	E	F
1		1999	2000	2001	2002	2003
2	Sales					
3	Marketing					
4	Admin					

Editing

Just as with navigating, selecting and formatting, a few tricks will make all the difference when you're editing an Excel spreadsheet.

Deleting cells, rows or columns

1. Select the cells, rows or columns you want to delete.
2. Right-click anywhere within the selection and select *Delete* from the shortcut menu, go to the *Edit* menu and select *Delete* or use the keyboard shortcut: *Ctrl + minus sign (–)*.
3. If you are deleting cells, Excel will ask you what you want to do with the remaining cells. Select from *Shift Cells Left*, *Shift Cells Up*, *Entire Row*, or *Entire Column*.

Adding cells, rows or columns

1 To insert cells, select the same number of cells immediately to the right or below of where you want the new cells.

To insert rows, select the same number of rows below where you want the new rows.

To insert columns, select the same number of columns to the right of where you want the new columns.

2 Right-click on the selection and select *Insert* or go to the *Edit* menu and select *Insert* or use the keyboard shortcut: *Ctrl + plus sign (+)*.

Adding or Deleting Entire Worksheets

- Right-click on the Worksheet name in the bottom left of the screen.
- Choose *Insert* or *Delete* from the *Shortcut* menu.
- To reorder worksheets, simply click and drag the worksheet name.

Inserting the time and date

To insert the current date into a cell press *Ctrl + semicolon (;)*.

Current time: press *Ctrl + Shift + semicolon (;)*.

Inserting a line break inside a cell

You would expect that pressing *Enter* would create a line break, but not in Excel. Pressing *Enter* moves to the next cell down, but there's a little-known trick to get a new line inside a cell: *Alt + Enter*.

Centring headings across columns

Sometimes you'll want to create a main heading that automatically centres itself across a range of columns. There is a feature in Excel called *Merge and Centre* which does just that.

- Type the heading into the far left cell, above your table of data.

- Select the cells across the data, starting from that far left cell.
- Click the *Merge and Centre* button on the formatting toolbar.

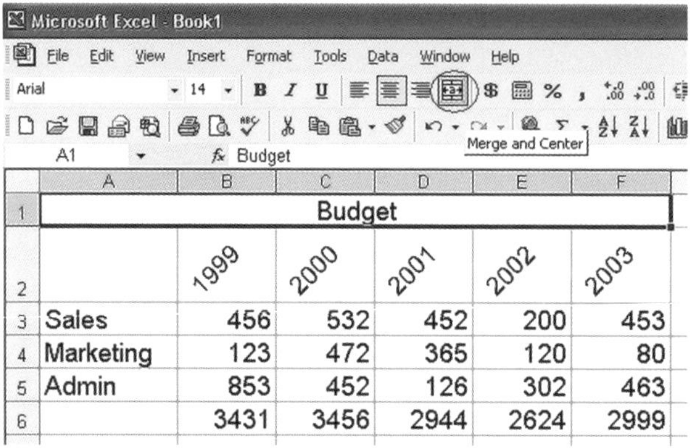

To insert the date and have it dynamically update each day, use the formula:

=today()

To insert a date a certain number of days in past or future, use *minus* or *plus* and the number of days. For example, to display the current date minus 25 days:

=today()-25

Swapping rows and columns

This function is for when you have already created your table of data, but you want to swap your row and columns around, and you want the data to follow.

- Select the data you want to change, including the row and column headings.
- Press *Ctrl* + *C* for *Copy*.

- Select a cell to start the *Paste* (it cannot be the same area we just copied, so go to a new sheet if you have to), and go to the *Edit* menu and select *Paste Special*. You may need to double-click the *Edit* menu to make *Paste Special* appear.
- Click *Transpose* and *OK*.

Printing

There are a few nifty tricks that you can use when printing large sheets within Excel that can make life a bit easier.

Page break preview

Ever wanted to have more control over the automatic page breaks? This 'big picture' view is a great function for just that. It zooms the page out, allowing you to see it all at once. Then you can move the page breaks around by simply dragging them with the mouse.

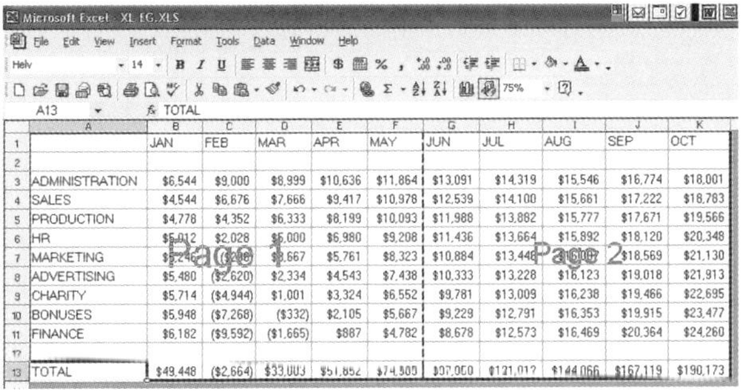

	A	B	C	D	E	F	G	H	I	J	K
1		JAN	FEB	MAR	APR	MAY	JUN	JUL	AUG	SEP	OCT
2											
3	ADMINISTRATION	$6,544	$9,000	$8,999	$10,636	$11,864	$13,091	$14,319	$15,546	$16,774	$18,001
4	SALES	$4,544	$6,676	$7,666	$9,417	$10,978	$12,539	$14,100	$15,661	$17,222	$18,783
5	PRODUCTION	$4,778	$4,352	$6,333	$8,199	$10,093	$11,988	$13,882	$15,777	$17,671	$19,566
6	HR	$5,012	$2,028	$6,000	$6,980	$9,208	$11,436	$13,664	$15,892	$18,120	$20,348
7	MARKETING	[illegible]	[illegible]	$[illegible].667	$5,761	$8,323	$10,884	$13,446	[illegible]	$18,569	$21,130
8	ADVERTISING	$5,480	($2,620)	$2,334	$4,543	$7,438	$10,333	$13,228	$16,123	$19,018	$21,913
9	CHARITY	$5,714	($4,944)	$1,001	$3,324	$6,552	$9,781	$13,009	$16,238	$19,466	$22,695
10	BONUSES	$5,948	($7,268)	($332)	$2,105	$5,667	$9,229	$12,791	$16,353	$19,915	$23,477
11	FINANCE	$6,182	($9,592)	($1,665)	$887	$4,782	$8,678	$12,573	$16,469	$20,364	$24,260
12											
13	TOTAL	$49,448	($2,664)	$33,003	$51,852	$74,305	[illegible]	[illegible]	$144,066	$167,119	$190,173

- Go to the *View* menu and select *Page Break Preview*. Automatic page breaks appear as blue dashed lines. Manual page breaks appear as blue solid lines.

- Move to one of the page breaks (horizontal or vertical) and drag it with your mouse to the desired location.
- To insert a page break, position your cursor below or to the right of where you want the page break and from the *Insert* menu, select *Page Break*.
- To remove a page break, drag it with your mouse to the grey area outside the worksheet while in Page Break Preview mode.

Print area

Sometimes you'll want only a particular part of your work-sheet to print. You can set a print area to do just that.

- Select the area you want to set as the print area using any of the techniques you've already learnt. For multiple areas, hold down the *Ctrl* key while selecting each block.
- From the *File* menu, select *Print Area* and *Set Print Area*.

The print area can be added to or cleared completely by going back to the *File* menu and selecting one of the options from *Print Area*.

Tip You can actually set the Print Area from within the *Page Setup* dialog box, too:

- Go to the *File* menu and select *Page Setup*.
- From along the top, select *Sheet*.
- Click in the *Print Area* box and then click the *Return to Worksheet* button on the right.
- Drag to select your print area on the worksheet and press *Enter* when finished.

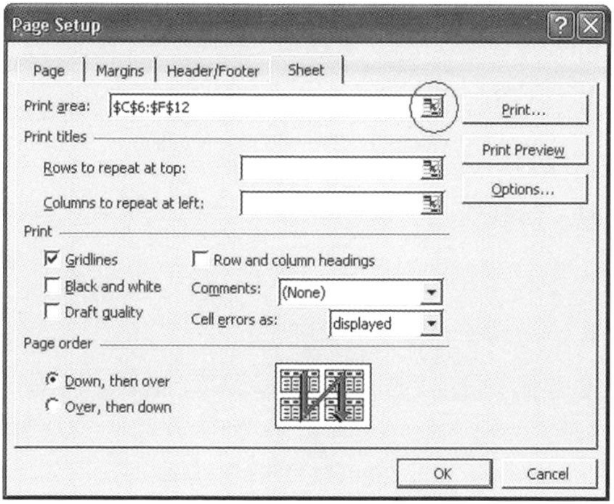

Repeat row and column headings

Worksheets often run across several pages, and you don't want to have to copy and paste your row and/or column headings to each new page, right? Well, here's yet another example of the magic of Excel.

- From the *File* menu, select *Page Setup*.
- Along the top, select *Sheet*.
- In the *Print* section, select *Row and Column Headings*.

Your row and column headings will now be automatically printed on each new page.

Other printing options

Now that I've got you into the *Page Setup* dialog box, have a look around at the other great functions you can make use of, such as:

- On the *Margins* tab – you can choose to centre your worksheet data horizontally or vertically.

- On the *Page* tab – you can fit your worksheet to a certain number of pages wide and tall (I use this quite often for worksheets that are just a little too big for one page).

Grouping sheets

Grouping sheets that are similar in layout will help you to make changes across all the sheets at the same time.

- To select more than one worksheet, select the first one by clicking once on the sheet name along the bottom of the screen and hold down the *Ctrl* key while you select each of the other worksheets.
- The tabs of the sheets selected appear in white.
- Click on any of the sheets in the group and make changes to it.
- The changes will appear on all of the sheets in the group.
- To ungroup the sheets, either right-click on one of the sheet name tabs and select *Ungroup Sheets* from the shortcut menu, or click on any other sheet within the workbook.

Creating a graph

Called charts in Excel, graphs are an unbeatable way to visually represent the numbers in a spreadsheet. Graphs that you create will automatically update if the original numbers change.

Quick graph

Another neat automatic feature of Excel is that you can create a graph from any data by clicking anywhere within that data and pressing the *F11* key along the top of your keyboard.

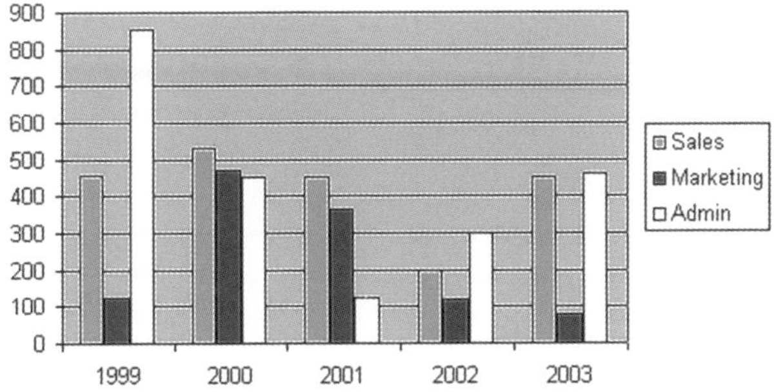

A standard graph (two-dimensional column graph) will be added to your workbook.

Fancy graph

If you want more control over the type of graph created, you will need to use the Chart Wizard.

- Click anywhere within or select the data you want to graph.
- Click the *Chart Wizard* toolbar button or go to the *Insert* menu and select *Chart*.
- Select your options from the Chart Wizard, answering the questions and clicking around the options, clicking *Next* and finally *Finish*.
- The graph will be embedded into your Excel spreadsheet.

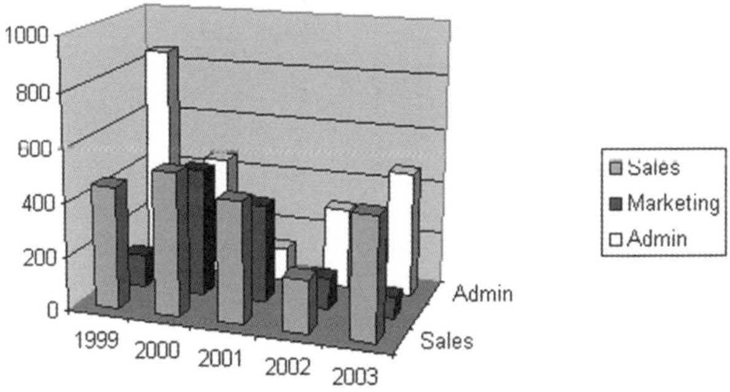

Freezing panes

Often, when a sheet takes up more than one screen and you need to scroll down, you don't want to lose the column and row headings off the screen. You can keep them at the top and left of the screen, to make things easier.

- Click underneath and/or to the right of where you'd like to freeze the screen.
- Go to the *Window* menu and select *Freeze Panes*.
- Scroll around in your sheet – you'll find that the headings won't scroll off the screen.
- To undo this, go back to the *Window* menu and select *Unfreeze Panes*.

Sorting

You can get Excel to automatically sort the data in a column or row by numerical or alphabetical order, and even in reverse order.

- Click anywhere in the column you want to sort by.
- Go to the *Data* menu and select *Sort*.
- If your list has a header row (headings), click the box marked *Header Row*.
- Select your sort criteria and click *OK*.

Microsoft PowerPoint

Why 'Slides'? The pages of your PowerPoint presentation are known as 'slides' because they were historically turned into 35mm slides for projecting to a large screen with a slide projector machine. You'll remember the slide projector machine if you think back to an early family slide night. How often did an upside-down slide appear? 'Ohhhh, Daaaaad!'

The most common frustrations with PowerPoint are usually about getting started – there seem to be so many options. Let's take a look at the best way:

Autocontent Wizard

It's a good idea to start your presentation using the Autocontent Wizard. This will make it much easier down the track to change formatting and layout across the whole presentation.

- From the *File* menu, choose *New*. The New Presentation Task Pane appears along the right of your screen.
- From the list of options, double-click on *From AutoContent wizard*

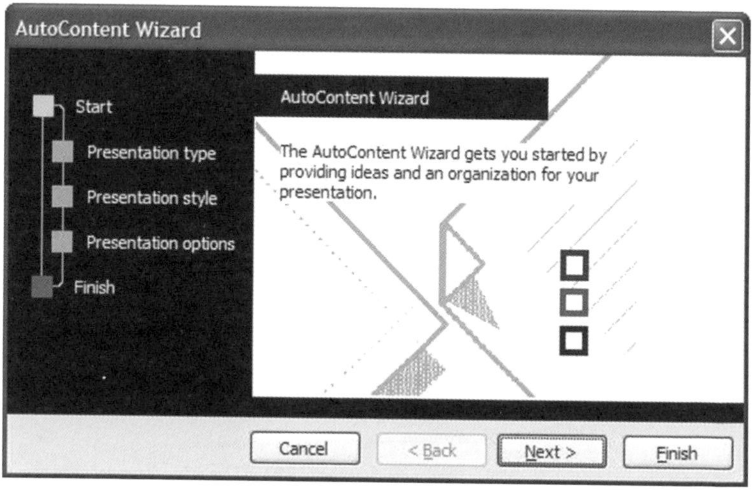

- Click *Next* to start answering the questions relating to the type of presentation you'd like to create.
- Click *Finish* when all questions are answered, then PowerPoint creates a sample presentation for you. It's a great starting point, so just go through and replace the text with your own!

Let's take a look at the slide show as it currently stands – press the *F5* key along the top of your keyboard, clicking the mouse to move through the slide show or *Esc* to return to the presentation.

Views

There are a few different ways to view your presentation as you edit it.

Normal View

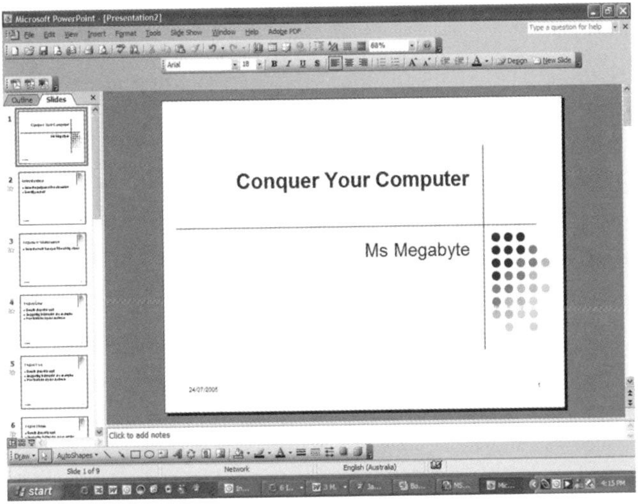

There are three useful parts to Normal View.

- The *Outline Pane*, where you edit and change the text in your presentation. Use the *Tab* key to demote a line of text (eg. from a bullet point to a sub-bullet point) and *Shift* + *Tab* to promote a line of text (eg. from a bullet point to a Slide title).
- The *Slide Pane*, which gives you a view of your actual slide. You can add extras like graphics and animation here.
- The *Notes Pane*, where you can type the speaker's notes that relate to each particular slide. (See down the bottom where it says 'Click to add notes'? Ever noticed that before? Most people haven't!)

You can drag the border between any of these panes to increase or decrease the size of them.

Slide Sorter View

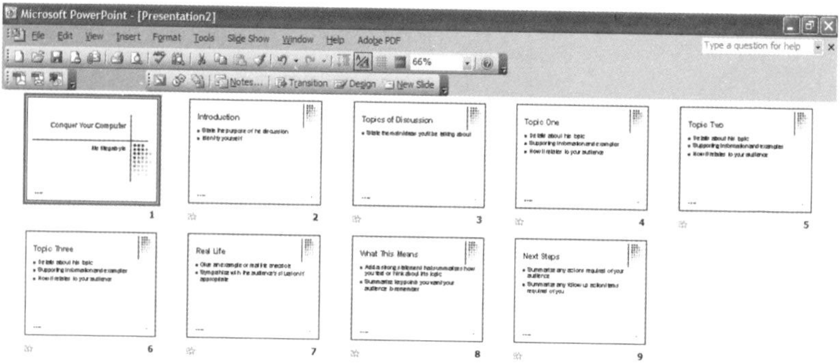

This is a great 'big picture' view of your overall presentation. In Slide Sorter view, you can:

- Select a group of slides by clicking the first one and holding down the *Shift* key as you click the last one.
- Select more than one slide at a time randomly by holding down the *Ctrl* key as you click each one.

- Move slides or groups of slides around by dragging them.
- Delete or copy slides or groups of slides.
- Use the *Slide Sorter* toolbar to add a slide or change the layout or design of one or all of the slides.

But mostly you'll use Slide Sorter view to set your special effects for the slide show. This is where you choose a Transition and Build animation. More on that later.

Slide Show

This button takes you into the show from the current slide (the keyboard shortcut is *Shift* + *F5*).

HOT TIP

To start the slide show from Slide 1 no matter what slide you're viewing, press *F5*.

Choosing a Design

Although you can choose a Design from any View, it's best to use Slide Sorter View. That way you get an instant look at the whole presentation.

- Go to *Slide Sorter View*.

- From the *Format* menu, select *Slide Design* to display the Slide Design Task Pane.

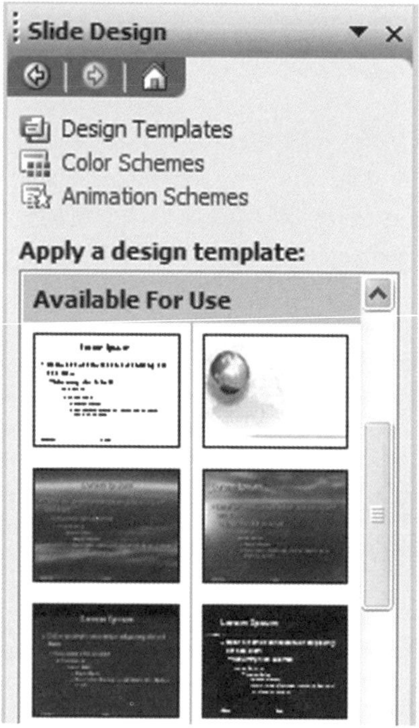

- Scroll through the different design templates, clicking on the ones you like to see how they look when applied to your own presentation.
- If you want to apply a design template to the selected slide(s), click the down arrow to the right of the template and choose *Apply to selected slides*.

Important: These designs can easily be used as just a starting point. If you find one that's almost right, choose it and we'll manipulate it later using the Slide Master.

Getting around your presentation

In Normal View:

- Use *Page Down* and *Page Up* to move from slide to slide
- With any object selected, use the *Tab* key to move to the next object on the slide. Use *Shift* + *Tab* to move backwards. This is a great way to find objects that may be hiding behind others. *Tab* until you have the hidden object selected, then use your arrow keys to nudge it out.
- Click and drag the scroll bar handle to the slide you want

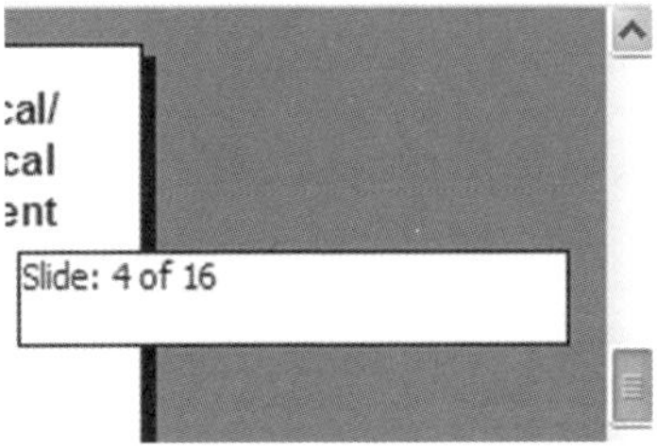

- Go to *Slide Sorter* view, then double-click the slide you want to view.

Editing tricks and tips

Most of the keyboard shortcuts you use in Word will work in PowerPoint, but here's a few I use most often:

- Double-click to select a word.
- If nothing is selected, *Ctrl* + *A* will select all objects.
- If a text box is active, *Ctrl* + *A* will select all text inside that box.
- *Ctrl* + *M* to insert a new slide.

- *Ctrl + D* to duplicate any selected object(s).
  (This also works in the Slide Sorter to duplicate an entire slide.)
- Add text to a shape by clicking the shape to select it, then typing out the text. For more tips on shapes, see the AutoShapes section in the Microsoft Office chapter.

Drawing tips

See the AutoShapes section in the Microsoft Office chapter.

Using the Slide Master

There is a 'template' behind your slides that can be altered easily to affect the layout of all slides. This is where you change the font, size, colour and position of the text for all slides. Delete unwanted objects from a design template. You can even add a logo on the slide master to have it appear on all slides.

Modifying a Slide Master

- Get to the Slide master by holding down the *Shift* key and clicking on the *Normal view* button in the bottom left corner of the screen (the first button). Click it again, without the *Shift* key, to get back to Normal view.

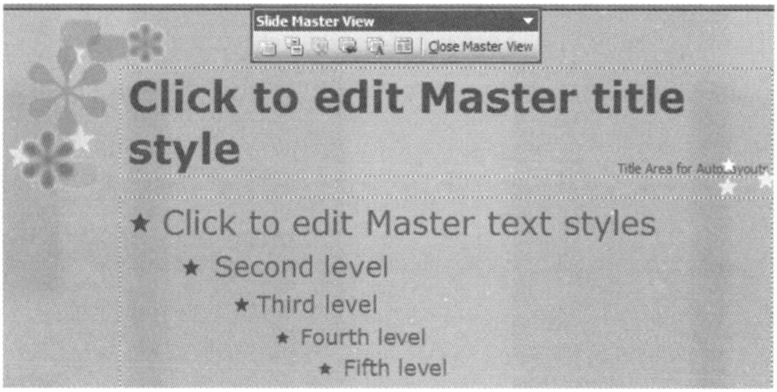

- Once in the Slide Master, you can treat the background graphics just as you would any piece of clipart. See the tips on manipulating clipart in the Microsoft Office chapter. Delete, recolour or resize any of the objects to suit.

Date, Footer and Number

You will notice that the standard presentation contains a Date, Footer and Number area in the Slide Master. Unless you don't need them, leave the placeholders there.

The <date/time> and <#> codes are designed to show the actual date/time and slide number automatically when you print or run a slide show.

Removing the master objects from just one slide

If you have a particular slide that doesn't lend itself well to the background objects on your Slide master, you can 'detach' that slide from the Master.

- Make sure you're in Normal view (not the Slide Master) by clicking the *Slide View* button in the bottom left corner of your screen (the first one).
- Make sure you're on the slide in question.
- From the *Format* menu, choose *Background*.
- Click in the box *'Omit background objects from Master'*.

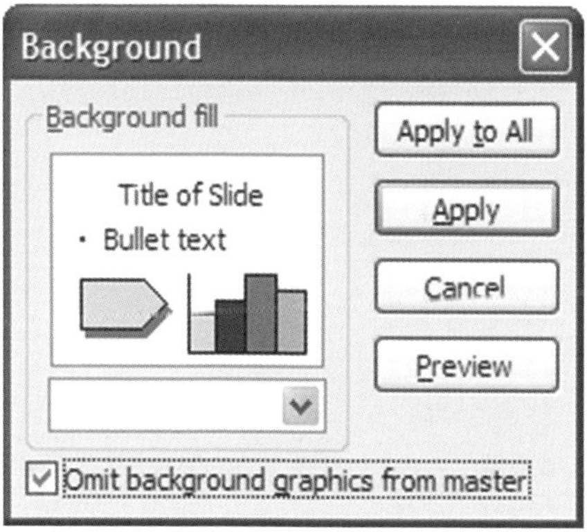

- Change the background colour to suit the slide – sometimes it's effective to have a plain white or black background if you're showing some large photos.
- Click *Apply*.

Adding the special effects

Most polished PowerPoint presentations are supported by effective animation which builds the bullet points one by one on each slide and a neat transition between each slide.

Choosing a Transition

- Click the *Slide Sorter* button in the bottom left corner of the screen (the one with the four windows).
- *Ctrl* + *A* to select all Slides.
- Locate the *Slide Sorter* toolbar, which sits immediately above your presentation slides.

- Click the *Transition* button to display the Transition task pane.
- As you click on the different transition options, you'll see a preview on all of your slides in the Slide Sorter window. To really see the transition in action, press *F5* to start your Slide show and click through it.
- The Transition task pane has a few other handy options – you can change the speed or add sound in the modify transition area. Or change the Advance slide settings if you want the slide to present itself!
- Turn off the AutoPreview if you find your screen is taking too long to preview each slide.

Animation

Remember the last presentation you sat through (or presented) where overhead transparencies were used on an overhead projector? There was a piece of paper over all but the first bullet point, which would be moved down manually, a point at a time, to stop the audience reading ahead? Too funny!

The essence of PowerPoint is the animation – you can control how your text and other objects appear on the slide during the slide show.

To apply animation to the bullet points on all of your slides:

- Click the *Slide Sorter* button in the bottom left corner of the screen (the one with the four windows).
- Make sure that at least one slide is selected by clicking once on one that has bullet points – we can apply the setting to the rest later.
- From the *Slide Show* menu, choose *Animation Schemes* to display the Slide Design – Animation schemes task pane
- Choose from the extensive options, clicking the *Play* button at the bottom to see a preview of the effect.
- Once you find one you like, click *Apply to All Slides*.
- Turn off the AutoPreview if you find your screen is taking too long to preview each slide.

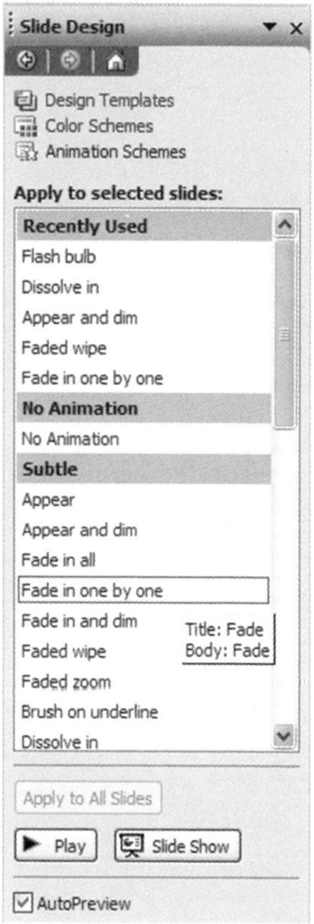

HOT TIP

- You can preview how the transition or animation will look for a particular slide by clicking the little star in the bottom left of the slide you want to preview (if you're in Slide Sorter view).

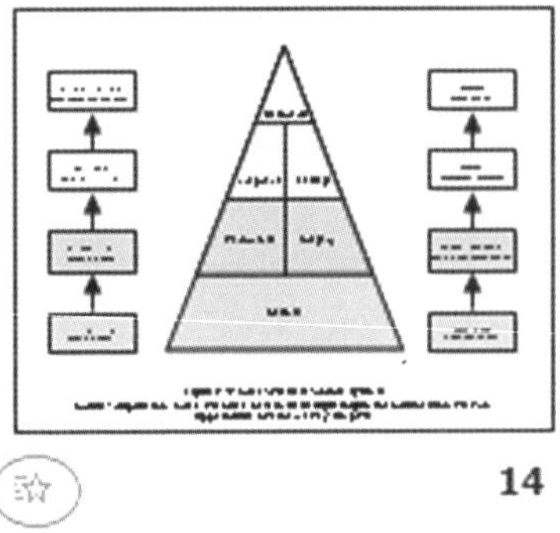

- To apply the transition only to certain slides, select them by holding down the *Ctrl* key and clicking each one, then apply the effect.

Slide show tricks

There are tons of shortcuts, but I've chosen the ones I think you'll use most often – remembering these is just a matter of practice, I promise!

- *Shift* + *F5* starts the show from the current slide.
- *F5* starts the show from Slide 1.
- *Shift* + *clicking* on the *Slide Show* button brings up the *Set Up slide show* options.

- *F1* during a slide show shows a list of shortcut keys which can be used during the show. (For example, pressing the letter *B* will black/unblack the screen – handy for when your meeting is going off on an important tangent and you need to come back to the presentation later.)
- If you move your mouse during a slide show, you'll notice the new *Slide Show* toolbar, which can be used to scroll back a slide and to select different pen options.
- Right-click (or *Shift* + *F10*) during a slide show for more options available from the shortcut menu.
- *Ctrl* + *S* during a slide show will bring up a slide navigator. Either double-click the slide number, type the number of the slide or arrow to it and press *Enter*.

Keyboard shortcuts for moving through slides during a slide show:

To the next slide	**To the previous slide**
N	P
Space or Enter	Backspace
Page Up	Page Down
Down arrow, right arrow	Up arrow, left arrow

To move to a particular slide number, *type* that number and press *Enter*.

Hidden Slides

If you're planning a presentation and you have some information you want to display only if you have time or a certain question is asked, you can include those slides but hide them, making them invisible unless you call upon them.

- Include the slides in your presentation wherever they are relevant.
- Go to *Slide Sorter View*.

- Select the slide to be hidden. For multiple slides, hold down the *Ctrl* key and select them all by clicking each one.
- From the *Slide Transition* toolbar, click the *Hidden Slide* button. (Or right-click on any of the selected slides and choose *Hide Slide* from the *Shortcut* menu.)

- During your Slide Show, you can display a hidden slide by pressing the *H* button from the slide before,
  OR you can type in the slide number and then *Enter*.
  OR you can right-click anywhere on the *Slide Show* and choose *Go to slide*. Your hidden slides will be displayed in the list with brackets around their number.

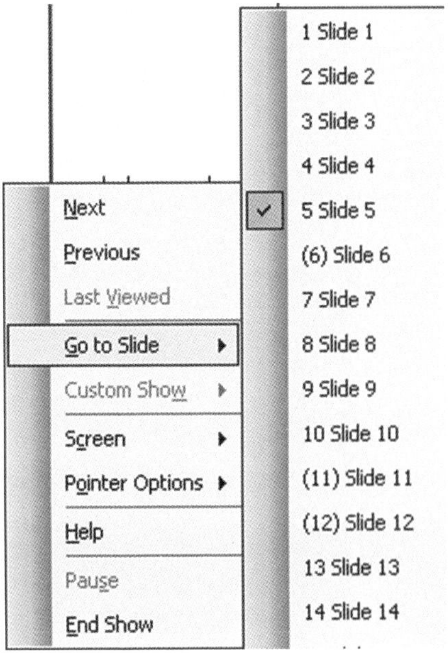

Printing

It's always very helpful to have a good look around the Printing options when you go to print. As your slides are often in quite large fonts, with only 6-8 bullet points on each slide, it will probably be overkill to print them one slide to a page for your audience.

Printing Handouts

In the *Print* box, locate the *Handouts* option, and choose that. 3 slides to a page is quite effective as it gives your audience space next to a small version of each slide in order to write notes.

See the tips below on printing 'pure' black and white, so you don't get the background shading.

Printing Notes pages

This is the best way to print your slides for your own use during the actual presentation.

You should use the Notes pages to include your own notes that jog your memory during your speech – you can even copy and paste your speech across from Word. But where to?

- You'll notice in Normal view that the very bottom of the screen has a horizontal grey bar.
- Grab that bar with your mouse and drag it up to about halfway.
- Click to add your speaker's notes.

Now, to print the Notes pages (which will include a small image of the slide they are connected to):

- Choose *File*, *Print*.

- Change *Print What* to *Notes Pages*.

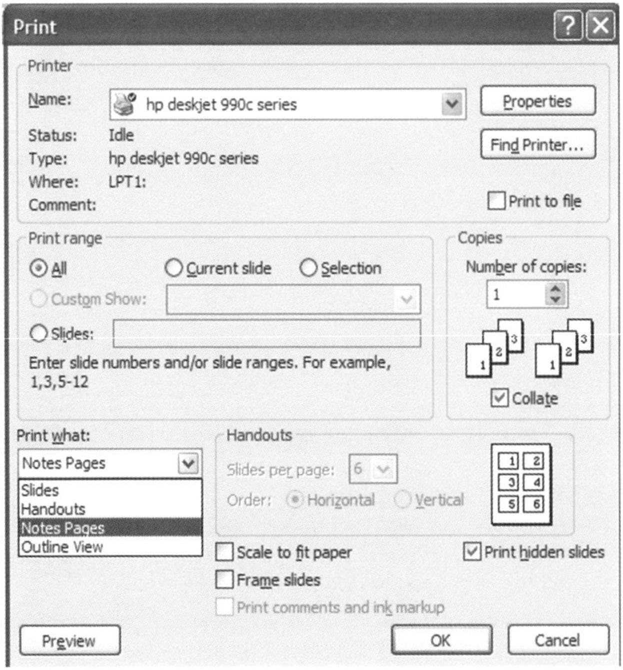

- Change *Colour* to *Grayscale*. (Or sometimes *Pure Black and White* is a better option depending on your printer, so print one first and see if you need to try the alternative.)

Saving as a slide show

You can save your presentation in the slide show format, which will make it start instantly in slide show mode whenever someone opens it. This is great for sending presentations to clients over email, or for giving the presentation away at a trade event on CD.

➤ From the *File* menu, choose *Save As*.

➤ From the *Save File as Type* box at the bottom, click the down arrow and choose *Powerpoint Show*.

File name:	figures.ppt	✔
Save as type:	Presentation (*.ppt)	✔

PowerPoint 95 (*.ppt)
PowerPoint 97-2003 & 95 Presentation (*.ppt)
Presentation for Review (*.ppt)
Design Template (*.pot)
PowerPoint Show (*.pps)
PowerPoint Add-In (*.ppa)

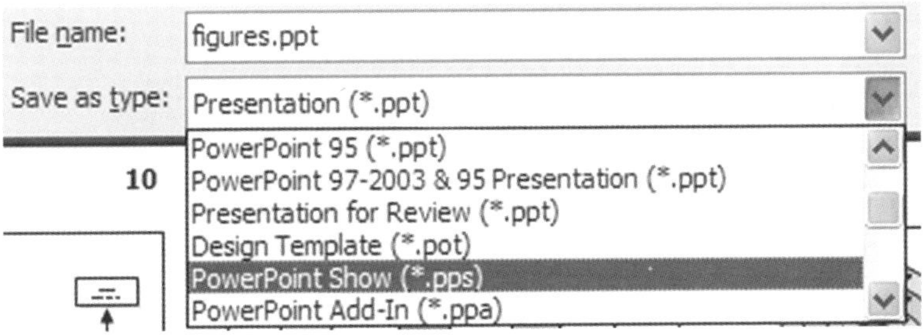

➤ When that file is launched, it will instantly go into Slide Show mode. When the *Esc* key is pressed, the file will close. The filename can be changed back to a 'ppt' for editing. (For tips on renaming files, see page 9.)

Handy hints for delivering your presentation

I've created and delivered at least 500 PowerPoint presentations, and I've sat through even more. These are the tips that will keep your presentations polished and professional.

➤ Don't overload your slides with bullet points – 6 is enough! If you have to use more, create a new slide with the same heading.

➤ Don't use different transition effects from slide to slide – choose an effective one and stick with it.

➤ Make sure your 'story' has a beginning, a middle and an end? First, tell them what you're going to tell them; second, tell them; third, tell them what you've just told them.

- Don't let the presentation be your speech. Use Power Point to SUPPORT your words by using only concise bullet points and relevant graphics.
- Spell check!
- Give good eye contact with the whole room, often.
- NEVER turn and talk at the projection screen. It's the cardinal sin of conducting PowerPoint presentations. Although the occasional glance at the screen is OK when you need a pause or you want to check the equipment, always face your audience.
- Be conscious of your umms and ahhs. Don't use them when you need a pause – use a PAUSE! There's nothing wrong with stopping for a few seconds. It actually grabs the audience's attention. Try it!
- Similarly, don't use 'essentially', 'basically', 'potentially' and 'actually'. Think about it – are they necessary, or are you just using them to pad out your sentence?
- And the best, most powerful tip of all? KNOW YOUR SUBJECT. If you're the expert on the topic you're presenting and you know your presentation well, you'll enter the room feeling confident and it will show.

Internet

Although its origins are deep in the 1960s, within the military, the Internet has been in common usage in Australia since only the mid 90s when around 40 million people in 150 countries were connected. It is estimated now that there are over 100 million people who use the Internet.

I came across a funny email the other day – it was one of those all-points bulletins that friends send around, and it had a link to a website which they recommended I click. I don't normally bother, but decided to take a look and was presented with a page that read simply: 'Attention please, you have reached the last page of the Internet.' When I went searching for it to put the address in this book, ironically, I found that there are now over 2,000 similar pages around the world, but here's an example:

home.att.net/~cecw/lastpage.htm

How websites work

Websites are assigned unique addresses, technically known as URLs. This stands for Uniform Resource Locator and is just like a street address for the Internet. A URL is made up of a few components separated by full stops. The address **www.asknow.gov.au** can be explained like this:

www	world wide web
asknow	domain name – usually the company or institution name
gov	type of organisation .com: commercial organisations; .edu: educational institutions; .org: mostly non-profit organisations; .gov: government departments; .net: traditionally for Internet-related businesses, but now more widely used .asn: associations;
au	country of origin (au=Australia; fr=France; uk=England, etc.)

Sites based in (but not restricted to) the USA don't have the last part of the address, e.g. **www.sony.com**; **www.disney.com**.

Other examples of URLs:
www.ninemsn.com.au
www.getmega.com
www.limerickpost.ie

As you can imagine, you could actually guess many Web addresses. If you're looking for the website of Village Cinemas in Australia, you'd type **www.village.com.au** and see what came up. If you're looking for the Google search engine in the US, you'd type **www.google.com** in the address field.

Automating common domain names

Don't leave home without: Whenever you want to visit a site that you know ends in a simple '.com' (not '.com.au' or '.co.uk'), type just the domain name (e.g. **symantec**) in the Address bar and then press *Ctrl* + *Enter*.

Internet Explorer will finish the address for you, adding both the www. at the start and the .com at the end. Try it!

Searching efficiently

The reason many people give up on the Internet is because they get frustrated with the amount of information they have to wade through to find the precious little bit they need.

Well, brush yourself off and let's have another go, because I'll absolutely guarantee that you'll never be frustrated when searching again – in a few paragraphs from now.

Firstly, use Google. It is the search engine located at **www.google.com** and it is still the easiest to use and most comprehensive search engine online today. In Australia, once you type **www.google.com** and press *Enter*, you'll get switched to **www.google.com.au**.

Other good search engines are:

- **www.webwombat.com.au** – Australia's oldest search engine, with a bit of everything!
- **www.ansearch.com.au** – with a 'power search' feature, allowing you to narrow down the search results in accordance with your gender and age group.
- **yahoo.com.au** – with a speedy 'local search' function, allowing you to find services and products in your local area.
- **www.sensis.com.au** – your search results are shown in a split screen with Australian results on the left and worldwide results on the right. You can then take your search into the White Pages, Yellow Pages or Trading Post by clicking the relevant button along the top.

Secondly, give a few moments' thought to what you're searching for. Is it information about a holiday to New York? Research for a school assignment on meerkats? Wedding celebrants in Sydney?

Thirdly, take a phrase from your search criteria and enclose it in quotes. Add any other words that will narrow down your search.

Let's assume I'm looking for a biography on the frontman from the Red Hot Chilli Peppers, Anthony Kiedis – something that includes information about his family. I go to **www.google.com** and type this:

"anthony kiedis" biography family

The quotes will tell Google to search for that phrase. Without them, Google finds pages with Anthony on them, pages with Kiedis on them, and then pages with Anthony Kiedis on them – so we'd have quite a bit to sift through.

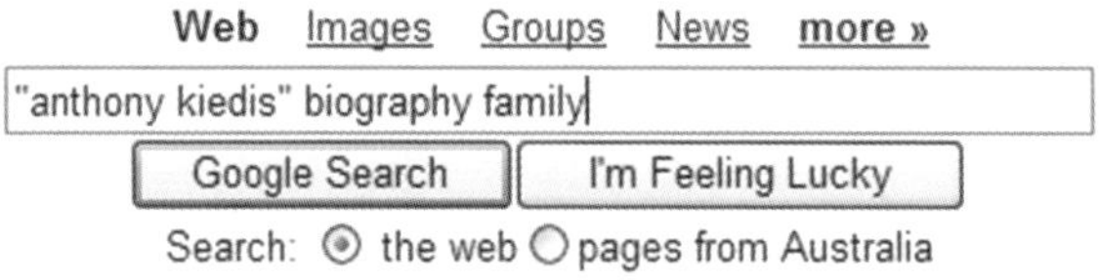

This tip would have to be the most popular thing I ever teach people about using the Internet.

Narrowing down by country

If you know that the site you're after is based in a certain country, narrow down your search even further by adding a site keyword in the search box, like this:

"male koala" lifespan site:au

Narrowing down by including and excluding

If it is essential that a certain word appear in your search results, put a plus sign (+) in front of that word, like this:

"male koala" lifespan site:au +zoo

If it is essential that a certain word does not appear in your search results, put a minus sign (–) in front of that word, like this:

"male koala" lifespan site:au +zoo –werribee, or

"banana cake" +chocolate –sultanas –eggs

Cool Google tools

Google Toolbar

Since I discovered the Google toolbar, I've never gone back to the Google homepage to do a search. Once installed, the toolbar sits at the top of your Internet Explorer window and you can do a quick search from it at any time.

- Go to **www.google.com**.
- Just above the search box, click the *More* link.

- Scroll down to Google Tools and click on Google *Toolbar*.

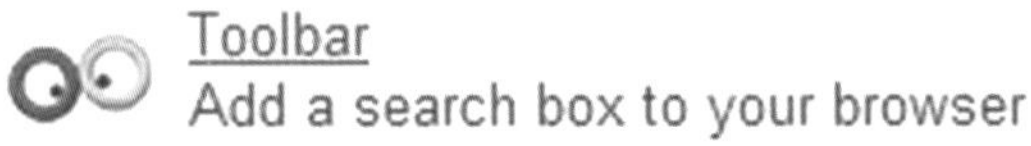

- Click the button to *Download Google Toolbar*.
- Click *Run* to run the installation immediately, or *Save* to save it to your computer and run it later.
- If you get a security warning from Windows, click *Run*.
- Choose your country (Australia!).
- Click *Agree* and *Continue*.
- Click to *Enable Advanced Features*.
- Click *Finish*.

Now your Internet toolbar has a new sibling. Here are some of the things you can do in the Google toolbar box:

- Type in your search keywords and press *Enter* instead of going to the Google homepage.

Google Search Features

These are some amazing ways you can use Google, either from the Google toolbar box or the Google homepage.

- A calculator! Just type your calculation and press *Enter* for the answer.

▼ A currency converter.

▼ Find products for sale by using **froogle.google.com**.

▼ Restrict your search to one website using the site search feature – say you want to look for information on kids games at my site:

| kids games site:www.getmega.com | Search |

Search: ⦿ the web ○ pages from Australia

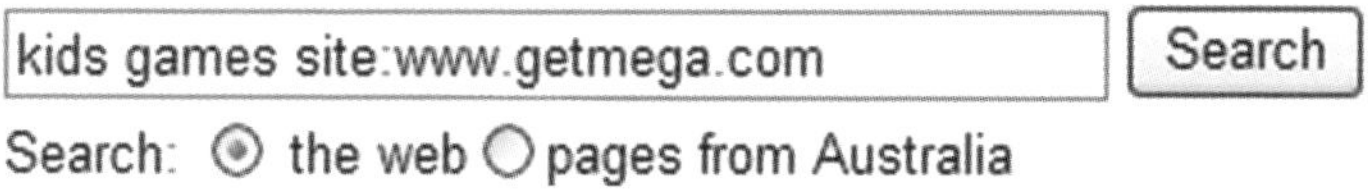

Setting your home page

The Internet site that comes up automatically when you start your Internet browser is called the home page and it is usually set to your computer's manufacturer's website or the website of the ISP you're signed up with. This is not usually of much use to you – it should be set to the website you visit most often, so change it! Here's the easiest way:

▼ Get into your browser and onto the Internet.

▼ Go to the website that you'd like to make into your home page.

For Internet Explorer:

▼ Go to the *Tools* menu and select *Internet Options*.

For Netscape Navigator:

▼ Go to the *Edit* menu and select *Preferences*.

For both:

▼ Click the *Use Current* button to set the home page to the current website or type in your own preference.

▼ Click *OK*.

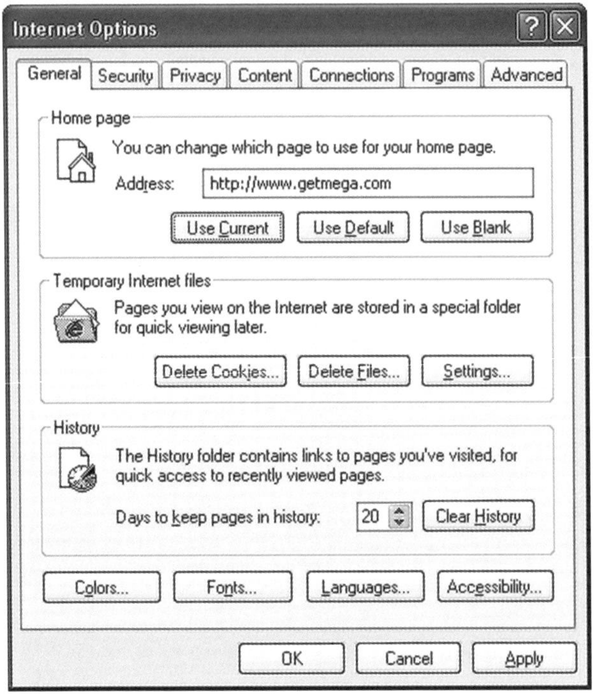

Managing Favourites

Because Internet Explorer is a US program, Favourites is spelt Favorites in the program, but we'll spell it correctly here.

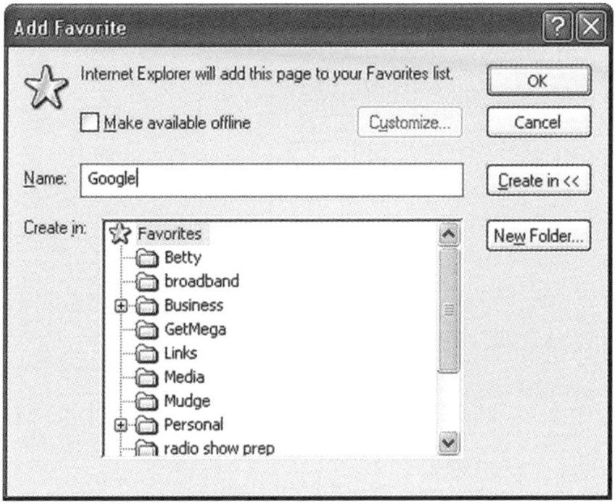

If there are sites you're visiting on a regular basis, it's time you saved yourself some time by adding the addresses to your list of Favourites. Then you'll be able to simply select the sites from a drop-down menu instead of typing the addresses out. You can even create folders for your favourite site names, keeping sites with a similar topic together.

The next time you've got a site on the screen that you'd like to add to your Favourites:

- Go to the *Favourites* menu and select *Add to Favourites*.
- Click *OK* if you simply want the site added to the bottom of the Favourites list.
- Click the folder name you'd like the site added to if you have one, then click *OK*.

- If there is not a suitable folder name, create one by clicking the *New Folder* button and typing a name. Then click *OK*.

Note Netscape Navigator users note that the equivalent to Favourites is Bookmarks.

Right-clicking

If you have already read the Word tips, you'll be a fan of this trick. The right-click works well in lots of Windows programs, but I would have to say that Internet Explorer is where I use it most.

You know those moments when you do a search for something on the Internet and you end up with a window containing a list of sites, of which you may very well like to visit four or five? You click on the first one, then get lost a few pages down that site, and you lose your original list – well, this technique will combat that.

- Next time you're looking at a list of search results, right-click on the first one you'd like to check out.
- A shortcut menu will appear at your cursor. Select *Open in New Window*.
- The new site will open in a brand new Internet Explorer window, leaving the original list in the background.
- To get back to the original list, use *Alt* + *Tab* (the task switcher).

Great Internet Explorer shortcuts

Keyboard shortcut	Function
F11	Full screen view on/off.
Alt + left arrow	Previous page.
Alt + right arrow	Next page.
Alt + D	Shortcut to get the address bar.
Ctrl + D	Adds current page to Favourites.
Alt + Home	Go to the home page.
Ctrl + F	Find on the current page.
F5	Refresh (useful when a page has stopped loading or you feel the page content is outdated).
Ctrl + F5	Refresh without checking if the page is old.
Ctrl + N	Opens a new Internet Explorer window.
Ctrl + left arrow	In the address bar, moves one logical step back in the address.
Ctrl + right arrow	In the address bar, moves one logical step forward in the address.
Ctrl + Enter	In the address bar, adds 'www.' to the beginning and '.com' to the end of text.

Printing from the Web

Printing from the Web can be very unpredictable. It usually depends on how the site is set up, and it is not easy to determine the results.

For best results, copy the part of the website that you want to print and paste it into a program that's a bit easier to manipulate, like Word.

- Click and drag over the part of the site you want to copy and paste into Word.

HOT TIP

If the text continues down the screen and clicking and dragging is proving difficult, first click your mouse at the beginning (you won't see a mouse cursor flashing, so just trust me), then scroll down and hold the *Shift* key down while you click at the end. All the text is now selected and you can move to the next step below. It gets easy after a little bit of practice.

- *Ctrl* + *C* to Copy.
- Switch to Word and click where you want the copied bit to go.
- *Ctrl* + *V* to Paste.
- If the text is still overly formatted, use *Ctrl* + *Z* to undo, and move to the next step.
- From the *Edit* menu, choose *Paste Special*.
- Double-click *Unformatted*.

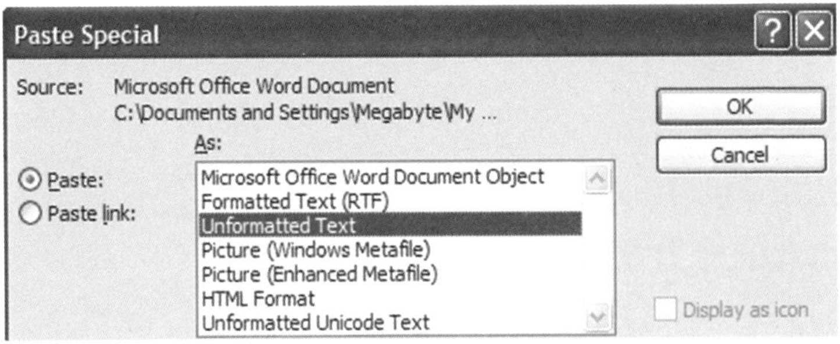

If it is a small part of the site that you're after, it would be easier to use the *Print Selection* technique in Internet Explorer.

- Click and drag over the bits you want, go to the *File* menu (or right-click) and select *Print*.

➔ In the *Print* box, find the *Print Range* options and select *Selection* and then click *Print*.

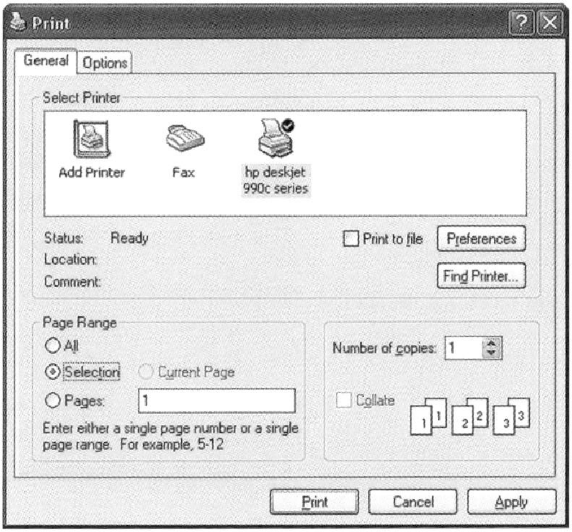

Chatting online – MSN Messenger

Your kids are likely to ask you if they can use Messenger before they've even used the Internet or created an email address. They spend all day at school together, but as soon as they get home they want to jump online and keep chatting. What about? Well, not much actually! A typical early teenage conversation is likely to go something like this:

minimegzie: *woz happenin*

agriffster: *not much*

minimegzie: *where did you get that icon?*

agriffster: *dunno*

minimegzie: *did you have a snack yet?*

agriffster: *noz*

minimegzie: *gtg byby*

agriffster: *kk c u*

So, what is Messenger?

It's a program that comes with Internet Explorer and usually runs in the background each time you turn the computer on. When you connect to the Internet, it starts up (unless you tell it not to, of course) and you can use it to see which of your friends are also online at the same time (they'll have a green icon alongside their names). You can then initiate a live keyboard chat by double-clicking their name.

Note If you don't have MSN Messenger installed, go to **messenger.msn.com** and download it.

Getting Started

Step 1 – Sign In

When you try to open Messenger, you'll be asked to *Sign In*. If you don't already have a Hotmail or MSN email address, you will need an MSN Passport – so click the *Get a .NET passport* link and follow the instructions to sign up.

Step 2 – Add Contacts

Now you'll need to populate your list of buddies, so click the + *Add a Contact* button at the bottom. Follow the instructions, entering your friends' email addresses. Messenger will check if they are current users of the program and if so, add them to your list. If not, you have the option of sending a message inviting them to sign up.

Step 3 – Chat!

- Check the little man icon to the left of your friends' names. If he's green, they are online right now. If red, they are offline.
- Double-click any names with green icons to open a chat window.
- Type a message and press *Enter* – it will appear in the chat window.
- As the friend starts to type their response, you'll be notified at the bottom of the screen.

Step 4 – Be brave ...

There are lots of fun things you can do with the latest version of Messenger. Here are a few to get started:

- Click the little smiley face just above your message entry window (next to the *Font* button) to use the 'emoticons'.
- Click the winking smiley face to use a more advanced emoticon.
- Choose a different background for your chat window.
- Click the last smiley face (with the funny face!) to 'nudge' the person you're talking to – they will hear a sound and their MSN window will wobble!
- Use the *Activities* button along the top to start a Whiteboard which you can both scribble on.
- Go to **www.netlingo.com/emailsh.cfm** and scroll down for a definitive guide to chat jargon, like:

m8	*Mate*
brb	*Be right back*
gtk	*Got to go*
lol	*Laughing out loud*
c u	*See you*
l8r	*Later*
imho	*In my humble opinion*

Step 5 – Protect yourself

- If there's someone you've added to your Contact list that you now would like to Block (so they can't tell when you're online), just right-click their name and choose *Block* from the shortcut menu.

Go to my Safe Surfing Tips on page 151 for lots more tips.

Beware

Sharing files is very easy with Messenger – during a chat, you click the *Send Files* button along the top toolbar, double-click the file you want to share and the other person clicks to accept it. This can leave you vulnerable to computer viruses attached to the transferred files, so be sure to have an up-to-date anti virus program installed.

The main problem I've found with a teenager using Messenger is that they'll download all manner of free novelty programs recommended to them by their Messenger friends. These programs can be very intrusive and messy, so it's important to make a policy that they ask your permission before accepting any files or clicking for any downloads.

Blogging

Short for the term 'web log', a blog is an online journal – a collection of entries published by the owner. The practice of blogging has really taken off, and you'll find a blog to cover every topic of discussion or interest. You'll even find some which are not of interest at all – even to the bloggers themselves!

The type of blog you might like to read will depend on your own interests – here's a cross-section of some interesting ones.

Celebrities

- RuPaul – **www.rupaul.com/weblog.shtml**
- Rosie O'Donnell – **www.rosie.com**
- Pamela Anderson – **pamelaanderson.blogs.friendster.com**
- Wil Wheaton – **www.wilwheaton.net**
- Moby – **www.moby.com**
- Bruce Willis – **www.brucewillis.com/notes/**

Interesting Australian blogs

- Looby Lu – **www.loobylu.com** is the home of a very talented Melbourne illustrator and toy maker named Claire Robertson ... follow the life of an interesting working mum with a small child.

LOOBYLU
Cold and cute
I haven't done anything crafty for the longest time. It's so cold in my studio that my finger tips turn blue and my feet feel like big lumps of solid wood in my sneakers.
I am also suffering from a slight case of blog fatigue which I am sure hits all of us from time to time. It's just too cold in here and of course Australian Idol has started so the couch is so much more inviting. Luckily I've been through this enough times now to know that these feelings of "oh, I wish I could just chuck it all in" will pass in a week or two.
Site contents
Archives
Out and About
A Month of Softies
Contact
Order Prints Online

- Gadget Lounge – **www.gadgetlounge.net** will keep you up to date with gadgets available in Australia
- My blog! **www.getmega.com/megablog**
- Travel Journals from around the world – **www.travelblog.org**

Starting your own blog

Interested in starting your own blog? Give it a go – there are tons of free tools you can use to get the job done. You can even update your blog instantly by emailing it or sending messages from your mobile phone ...

www.blogger.com: just create an account, come up with a name for your blog, choose from one of the many fantastic design templates and start writing!

spaces.msn.com: using an MSN Passport (if you don't have one, sign up for free), you can create your own space for your blog and include a photo gallery and more.

Newsgroups and message boards

There is a wealth of untapped information out there on the Internet. Newsgroups and message boards are communities full of like-minded people discussing their topic in all manners, from calm and relaxed to heated and fervent! They are free and work kind of like graffiti – someone writes a message and others respond to it. Some of them are not moderated, so beware – you could see some comments that may offend.

Newsgroups

All you need is a newsgroup reader, and luckily there is one that comes with the latest version of Outlook Express. Most ISPs offer a news server and will tell you what it is called, or you may find the information on their website. When you have those details:

- Open Outlook Express and go to the *Tools* menu, then select *Accounts*.
- Along the top, click *News* and then *Add News*.

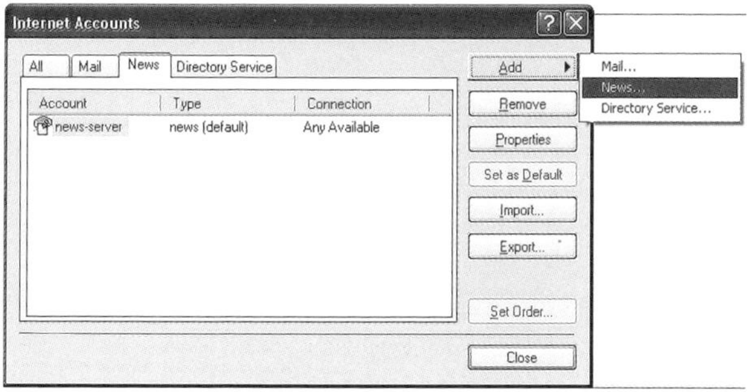

- Decide on a display name that will be used to identify you in the newsgroups. If you think you're going to want to remain anonymous, make up a name. (If you are going to post anonymous messages, please be responsible!) Click *Next*.
- If you want to give out your email address, type it in the *Email Address* box; otherwise you can leave it blank or type any character there. Click *Next*. (Say yes if Outlook asks you if you want to use the address you've typed, even if it is wrong).
- The next screen asks for the name of the news server you want to use. You will need to get this from your ISP. It is likely to be something like **news.ozemail.com.au** or **news.bigpond.com**. Click *Next* and *Finish*.
- Now you need to find some newsgroups to subscribe to! Click the *Newsgroups* icon and a list will appear. Type a topic you're interested in into the box at the top, such as **television**.

- You'll find many options will appear – select one by clicking *Subscribe* and *OK*.

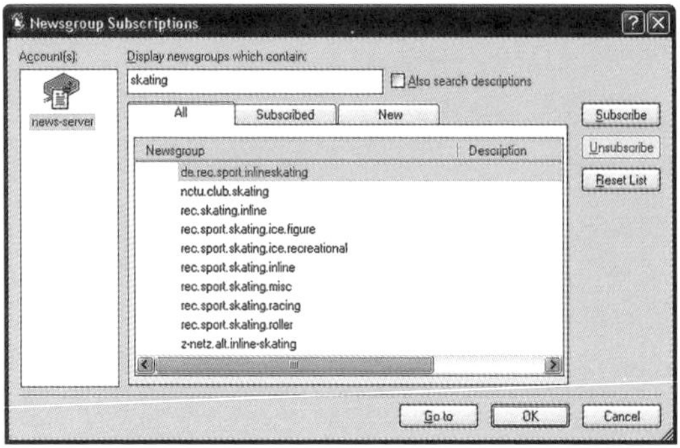

- Click on the name of your newsgroup in the left window and the last few weeks' messages will appear for you to browse through.
- Post your own message by clicking *New Post* or reply to others by clicking *Reply Group*.

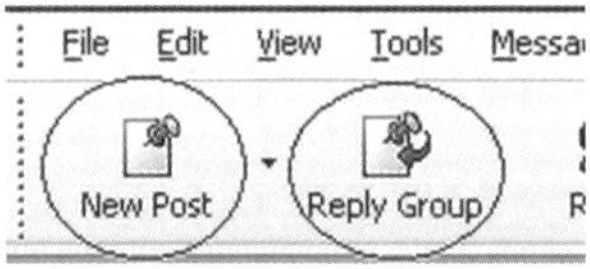

Have fun!

Message boards

These work the same way as newsgroups, but the messages are displayed on a website, so a news reader is not required.

The best example of a message board would have to be my own of course! I created it because I was getting so much email from people needing help with their computers. I wanted people to post their questions in a public place, so that others could benefit from the answers.

The GetMega Helpdesk has thousands of questions and answers to trawl through, and computer users of all abilities ask questions and give answers 24 hours a day. As it turns out, I hardly ever answer the questions myself because there are some terrific helpers out there in cyberspace who do it for me. And I've never even met them! Thanks Jimbob, Jeffery and Tassie!

Help Desk

Forum	Topics	Posts	
Computer help Computer and Internet support area. Discuss software (including Microsoft Office), hardware and Internet related issues. Moderator Managers	2244	14137	:
Viruses/Pop-ups/Firewalls/Security Area to get familiar/aware about Viruses, Pop-ups, Firewalls, Internet Security and how to protect yourself from such nuisances. Moderator Managers	306	1445	M
Notifications on Updates and Patches Area to inform members of Security related Updates and software upgrades. Moderator Managers	15	66	:
How-To's and FAQ's Useful information and answers to the most commonly asked questions. Moderator Managers	57	62	T

You will need to register to start asking questions, but it's free!

www.getmega.com/helpdesk

To find other message boards, try using **www.google.com**. For example, if you're looking for message boards about weddings, go to Google and type in:

"message boards" wedding

You'll be trawling through the results for ages!

Pop-up advertisements

You will be pleased to know that there is a way to stop those annoying pop-up advertisements appearing on top of your Internet browser. It involves downloading a bit of software, and there are lots of free programs to choose from.

Go to **shareware.cnet.com** and type **popup killer** in the search box and you'll be presented with all of your options. It is best to try out a few, one at a time, to see which one suits your Internet surfing best.

Don't forget that your anti-virus software may very well come with an ad-blocking component. I'm using Norton Internet Security and I have killed my pop-up advertisements successfully with the inbuilt ad-blocking function.

If a certain site has taken over your web browser and appears as your home page, you'll need to reset your home page by following the instructions at the beginning of this chapter.

Spyware

As you surf the net, register on websites and download various utilities, Spyware will get installed on your computer. Not always nasty, Spyware keeps track of your internet viewing habits – usually in order to show you targeted advertising.

It's a good idea to give your PC a good clean-up occasionally.

The free version of Ad-Aware is the most popular industry standard for detecting and removing SpyWare, so grab it from:
www.lavasoft.de/support/download.

Copyright

The Internet is like a huge public library. When you want a copy of something, you don't have to hide from the librarian and sneak to the photocopier – you can just drag your mouse over it, right-click on it, select *Copy* then paste it into Word.

But, is it yours to do with it as you will? The short answer is no. In Australia, copyright is automatic and material does not require a © symbol to be protected. If you want to use anything from a website that is not yours, you should seek permission from the owner of that content.

Although created for educational institutions, the invaluable documents and templates at the SofWeb site will help you with copyright issues:

www.sofweb.vic.edu.au/internet/copy2.htm

Useful sites

www.google.com – not just the normal search, but try clicking along the top of the search box on *Images* and *News*, both self-explanatory.

www.wishlist.com.au – a gorgeous collection of gifts for any occasion, offers gift wrapping and personalised cards.

www.ninemsn.com.au – Australia's most visited one-stop shop, including info on all of the Channel 9 shows, news, shopping, and too much more to mention.

www.rosesonly.com.au – gorgeous flowers, delivery same-day and not too expensive.

www.getmega.com – of course!

www.choice.com.au – the Australian Consumer Association's website where you can purchase articles one at time, as well as view many free articles.

www.asknow.gov.au – a relatively new initiative by libraries all around Australia – you visit the site and ask any question at all in a window on the right. In the left-hand side of the screen, a librarian will show you how to find the answer on the web. Try it – it's like magic!

www.yahoo.com.au – excellent portal with a good website directory, free email, news, shopping and other stuff.

www.abc.net.au – excellent for up-to-date Aussie news, and try the rest of the site out, especially the kids section.

www.shareware.com – a one-stop shop for searching for downloadable programs online.

www.echoice.com.au – home loan comparison site for Australians.

www.iselect.com.au – similar to above, but for health insurance comparisons.

www.sensis.com.au – the home of the Yellow Pages; White Pages; Whereis, which gives you driving directions; Citysearch, a lifestyle guide, and more.

www.fairfaxdigital.com.au – home of the *Sydney Morning Herald*, *The Age*, the *Financial Review*, Trading Room and Money Manager.

www.colesonline.com.au – shop online for your supermarket staples.

www.woolworths.com.au – same as above.

Kids' safety

The Internet is packed to the rafters with material, some unsuitable for kids – and most adults too, come to think of it! This all comes from the Internet's tendency to allow free speech without any sort of big-brother regulation. So how do we protect the kids without being so strict that they learn to loathe using the PC?

Built-in controls

Internet Explorer and other browsers have some built-in tools to filter out the rubbish.

- Go to the *Tools* menu and select *Internet Options*.
- Click *Content* along the top.

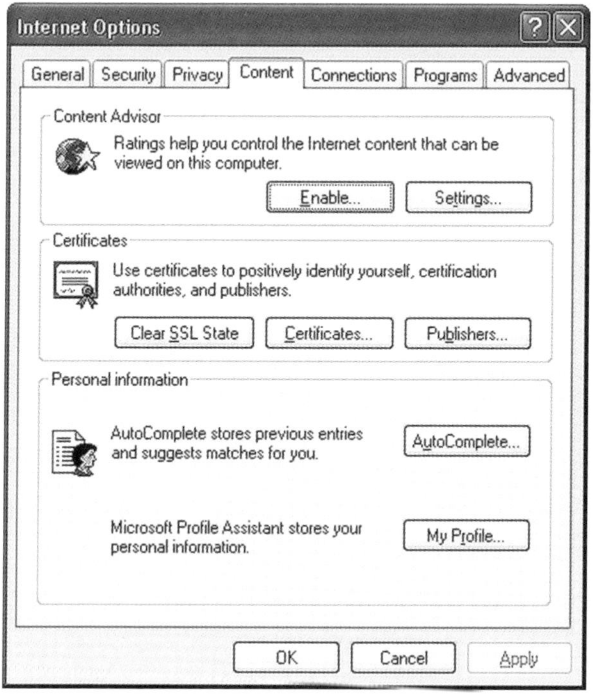

- In the *Content Advisor* section, click *Enable*.
- Customise the *Ratings* settings to suit yourself, using the slider to specify the level of protection.

- Click *OK* and enter a password that will be required to turn the *Content Advisor* off. Do not forget this password!
- To change the password, you'll need to go back to the *Content Advisor* and select the *General* section, then select *Change Password*.

Extra software

You can select software and even Internet service providers, who will give you an extra level of filtering and security.

Norton Internet Security comes with some good parental control options within the software. You can set up different user accounts for the computer, with different access rights for each person. It also comes with a personal firewall, which protects your computer from unwanted advances. Available from your local software retailer for around $150.

The Australian Broadcasting Authority (ABA) has some comprehensive information available online about selecting a filter and a link to their research paper on effectiveness – visit it at:
www.aba.gov.au/internet/overview/filtering.shtml

The ABA also has a terrific website which gives cybersmart tips for kids, parents and teachers – visit it at: **www.cybersmartkids.com.au**

www.netalert.com.au is Australia's Internet Safety Advisory Body and the site has tons of information about Internet filters and keeping kids safe.

And for even more tips on keeping kids safe online, visit:
microsoft.ninemsn.com.au/protectyourkids.aspx

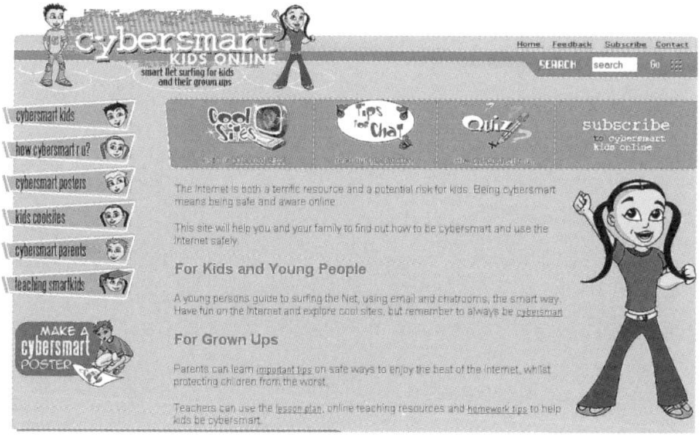

Mega's safe surfing tips

1 Put the PC in the busiest room of the house – don't let kids hide in their room where you can't supervise.

2 Make it your mission to close the 'knowledge gap' – you cannot supervise kids unless you know how to use the Internet yourself.

3 Educate kids not to give out any personal details – just like normal stranger-danger.

4 Explain what to do if they see something that makes them uncomfortable – have a policy where they have to turn off the monitor and come and get you.

5 Use parental controls, both built-in and bought software, as mentioned above.

6 Check your child's school for their policies and integrate them into your own home.

Great kids' sites

www.yahooligans.com – another bookmark-worthy site for kids.

www.matmice.com – kids' site for creating their own websites, created and maintained by kids.

www.sesameworkshop.org/sesamestreet – a really engaging, fun and educational site. Elmo's World is a particular favourite in our house.

www.abc.net.au/children – a well-illustrated site full of TV favourites.

www.ajkids.com – the Ask Jeeves search engine for kids, where you can ask a question in plain English!

www.etch-a-sketch.com – yes, there's an online Etch-a-Sketch, and you can use your keyboard arrows to draw. There are lots of other games and colouring pages, too.

www.seussville.com/university – you'll have 'lots of great fun that is funny', as you can guess, I profess!

www.nickjr.com – Blue's Clues, Dora, Miss Spider, Franklin: you name it, there'll be some fun to have!

www.pingu.net – 'mahrp mahrp'!

Cleaning up

Cookies

Cookies are small bits of information that websites store on your computer that can be retrieved automatically later. It may sound a bit intrusive, but they can actually be quite helpful. A former Netscape programmer, Lou Montulli, is credited with inventing the cookie, and I'm guessing the name came from the little bits of cookie that Hansel and Gretel left behind in the forest when they got lost! Lou also created The Amazing FishCam, the Internet's second-ever 24-hour-a-day live web camera and he has a site at **www.montulli.org/lou**

There are some sites that you visit often that require information about you in order to proceed, like home-shopping sites, subscription-based sites, and membership-only sites. If some of the information, like your username or membership number is stored on your computer by that website, it can be retrieved later to save you typing it in again.

Cookies are also used as a way of showing you different advertisements when you visit a website. The website stores information about the ads it has displayed to you, so it can change them next time you visit.

Cookies cannot be accessed by sites that did not create them.

You can delete and clear the cookies at any time without causing any problems beyond the fact that you'll have to enter information into some web forms again.

Deleting cookies in Internet Explorer

- From the *Tools* menu, select *Internet Options*.
- On the *General* tab, click *Delete Cookies* then click *OK* to confirm.

Temporary internet files

Sometimes Internet Explorer can misbehave – pages won't load or refresh properly, you seem to lose your internet connection or can't close a window. In this instance, it's a good idea to clear out the Temporary Internet Files (these are the files your computer saves so pages will load quicker the next time you need them).

- From the *Tools* menu, choose *Internet Options*.
- On the *General* tab, select *Delete Files*, click *Delete all offline content* and click *OK*. This could take some time if you haven't done it for a few months and you're a heavy internet user, so be patient.

History

If you share your computer with others, it might be useful to know how to clear the History which pops up as you start typing Internet addresses in the address bar, or when you click the down arrow to see what's been visited recently.

- From the *Tools* menu, choose *Internet Options*.
- On the *General* tab, select *Clear History* then click *Yes* to confirm.
- Close Internet Explorer and re-launch it to check the History list is gone.

AutoComplete

There is a feature in Internet Explorer that will remember your information as you fill out forms on the Internet and automatically complete them for you next time.

To clear your personal information:

- From the Tools menu, select *Internet Options*.
- On the Content tab along the top, click *AutoComplete*.
- Click *Clear Forms*.

eBay

What is it?

eBay is a huge Internet market that was founded in 1995 and came to Australia four years later. Think of something you might like to buy or sell. Go on – close your eyes and think of something. Yep! You can buy and sell THAT on eBay!

Best of all? It's surprisingly easy to use. I dare you.

From your favourite TV series to collectible whirligigs, MP3 players to ballet tutus, it's all here. The most expensive item ever sold on eBay was a $AUD4.9 million dollar private jet!

I've sold things from a cardboard box (with the Chanel logo on it) to a set of 2nd hand bi-folding laundry doors (which were then shipped from Melbourne to Qld). I've bought things like an empty Wallace and Gromit bubble bath statue and a 1st edition H.G. Wells book. There are over 135 million registered users of eBay all around the world and over 44 million items listed at any one time. Don't let that scare you though – I promise it's actually fun, easy to use and delightfully addictive.

On the Australian site, a car is sold every 40 minutes, a baby item every 10 minutes, a toy every 30 seconds and a piece of women's clothing every 18 seconds.

In a nutshell:

To buy on eBay

- Search for an item you want.
- Register.
- Try to make the highest bid.
- Pay by direct debit, credit card, cheque or money order.

- Receive your item.
- Leave feedback for the seller.

To sell on eBay

- Take good photos of your item.
- Register.
- List it, using special features to make it stand out.
- Start the auction and await the highest bidder.
- Receive funds and post the item.
- Leave feedback for the buyer.

Fees

Always check for current prices at **http://pages.ebay.com.au/help/sell/fees.html**. Buyers don't pay fees to eBay. Sellers pay:

- An insertion fee of $0.30 – $3.50 depending on the auction's start price.
- For vehicles and real estate, there are fixed fees of $5 and $75 respectively.
- If the item is sold, a final value fee of:
  5.25% of the final price to $75,
  + 2.75% of the remaining final price to $1000,
  + 1.50% of the remaining price.

  eg: Item sells for $1300.

$75 x 5.25%	=	*3.94*
+ $925 x 2.75 %	=	*25.43*
+ $300 x 1.50%	=	*4.50*
TOTAL	=	*$33.87*

- For motorbikes, there is a fixed fee of $30, cars and other vehicles are $40 and there is no fee for real estate.

Getting Started

Note See eBay Terminology at the end of this chapter.

Get a PayPal account

www.paypal.com.au

As PayPal is a common payment method across eBay, I recommend signing up for a free account, although it's not absolutely necessary.

PayPal allows anyone with an email address to make or receive payments over the Internet. It keeps your sensitive credit card and bank account details private and is an easy, quick payment option.

Use PayPal for selling on eBay:

- Add PayPal as the payment option in your listing, and the winning bidder can pay instantly from their own PayPal account or credit card.

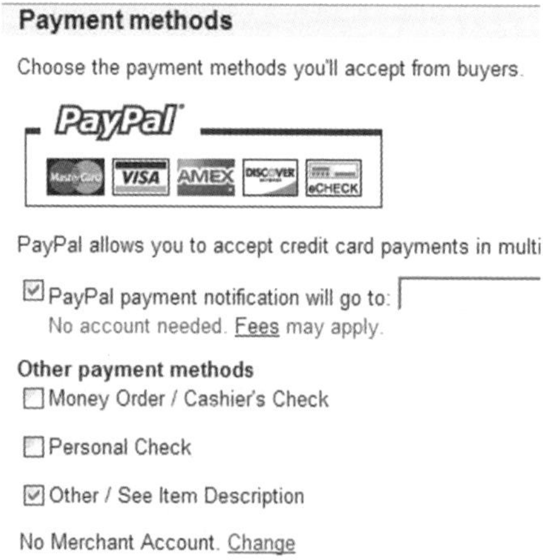

- Pay a small percentage (from 1.4%, depending on your volume of transactions).

Use PayPal for buying on eBay:

- It's free and the seller never sees your personal account information.
- Click the *PayPal* icon when the auction ends.
- Pay with your credit card (you don't even need a PayPal account to do this), or
- Pay with money from your PayPal balance (you can transfer money into your PayPal account from your own bank account). If your PayPal balance is insufficient, PayPal will use the credit card you have linked to your account.
- List different credit cards and bank accounts with PayPal, and choose a different one each time.

Getting the cash: You can withdraw funds from PayPal any time back to your bank account. Fees apply for certain amounts ($1 to transfer less than $150). Note that the funds can take up to 7 days to appear in your account.

Setting up a PayPal account

1. From the **www.paypal.com.au** page, click *Sign Up*.
2. Select *Personal Account*, making sure the country selected is *Australia*, and click *Continue*.
3. Fill out the form with your personal details.
4. Scroll down to set up the secret question.
5. Scroll down again to view and accept the statements and policies.
6. Type the security code shown in the box – don't use any spaces and make sure you enter the code exactly as shown, including capital letters.
7. Press *Enter* or click the *Sign Up* button at the bottom.

8 Enter your credit card details now, or you can do this bit later by clicking *Cancel*.

9 Now, go to your email program and check for an email from PayPal.

10 Click on the link in the email to verify your registration, confirming your email address.

11 Now you can use your PayPal account to send money to or request money from anyone with an email address.

Register on eBay

You can browse and search on eBay without registering, but if you want to bid, buy or sell, you'll need to sign up. It's free!

➚ Go to **www.ebay.com.au** and click *Register*.

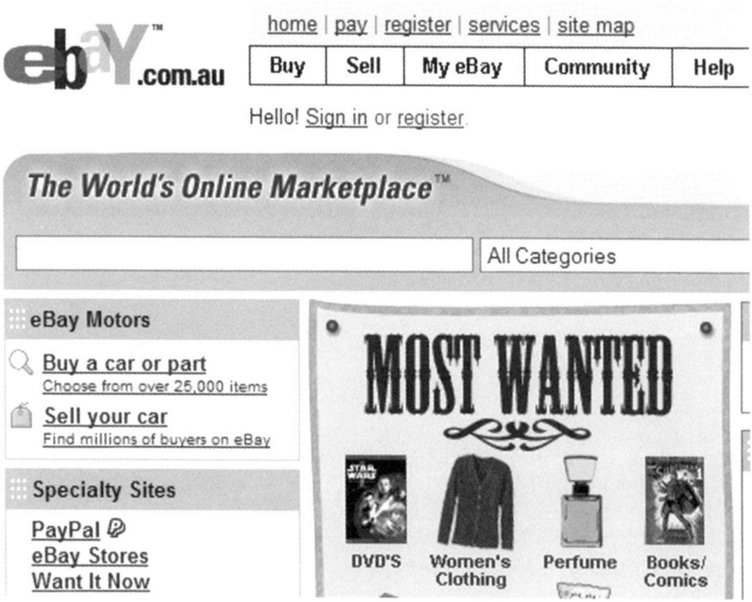

- Fill out the form, check out the User Agreement and Privacy Policy (has anyone ever actually read one of these from top to bottom?!), tick the boxes and click *Continue*.
- Choose a suggested eBay ID, or create your own and fill out the rest of the form, then click *Continue*. eBay will send you an email message to confirm your registration.
- Now, go back to your email program and check for new messages. Open the email from eBay – then follow the instructions in the email by clicking *Complete eBay Registration*.
- eBay may now ask you to create a Seller's Account. I suggest you try buying something first, to see how the whole process works. When you're ready to sell something, jump straight to that section on page 178.

Set up Email folders

As you increase your eBay activity, be sure to set up a good filing system in your Email program. See our chapter on Email for tips on creating folders.

Microsoft Outlook

- Create an *eBay* folder by clicking on your Inbox and using the shortcut *Ctrl + Shift + E*.
- Within the *eBay* folder, create a *Buying* folder and *Selling* folder.
- Within the *Buying* folder, create folders for *Items Won, Items Paid For, Items Received, Items Complete*.
- Within the *Selling* folder, create folders for *Items Listed, Items Paid For, Items Complete*.

Learn to use multiple windows

Window switching

When buying and selling, it's really helpful to have more than one Internet window open at a time and switch between them. In one window, you'll be listing a computer game you want to sell and in the other you'll be searching the net for a good description of it (don't forget to credit the site you lift the info from). More commonly, you'll be using different parts of eBay in the separate windows.

- Open your Internet browser and go to **www.ebay.com.au**, logging in if required – then click the *Buy* button along the top.
- *Ctrl* + *N* to open a new window. Now you have two Internet browser windows open, with the same Buy page loaded.
- On this second page, click the *Sell* button.
- Now, to go back to the Buy page, hold down the *Alt* key and press *Tab* once (DON'T hold *Tab* down – just press it once), then let go of both keys immediately.
- Try it again – *Alt* + *Tab*, and again, and again – you'll see you can easily switch between the two open windows.

Copy and Paste from one window to another

- Click and drag over the info you want.
- *Ctrl* + *C* for copy.
- *Alt* + *Tab* to the window you want to copy into.
- Click where you want the copied text/graphics to go.
- *Ctrl* + *V* for paste.

My eBay

Clicking on the *My eBay* link at the top of any page will take you to a page that acts as a one-stop shop for your bidding, selling, watching, feedback and account preferences.

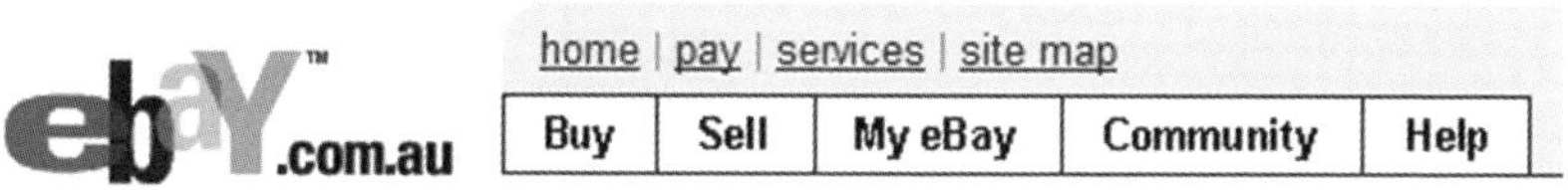

At a glance you'll get a summary of your eBay activity. Use the *My eBay Views* vertical menu along the left of the page to find everything you need.

You can even add your favourite sellers and search criteria to the list, making it easier to jump straight to them later.

To add a common search to your list of favourites:

- Conduct the search by entering your keywords and clicking the *Search* button
- In the top right corner of the search results, click the link *Add to Favourites*.
- On the next screen, choose your preferences – eg: you can have eBay email you whenever a new item appears that matches your keywords.
- Click *Save Search*.

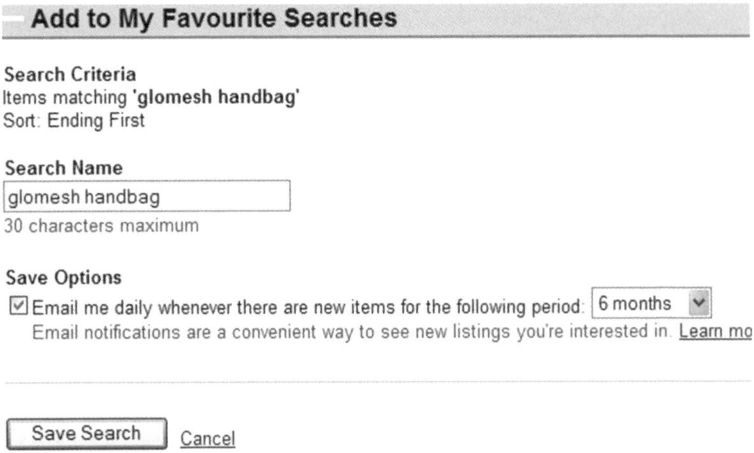

To change the order of the summaries, or even add/remove them, click the *Customise Summary* link at the top right of the list.

Buying

Hold on to your mouse pads! Prepare to become secretly addicted to the pleasure that is eBay. Sure, it's possible to stay away from it for weeks at a time, but once you come back, you're hooked for days!

Finding items

Search

The quickest way to find what you're after is to type a keyword into the search box in the top right corner of most pages.

For example, if you're looking for baby boy clothes, size 00, type: **size 00 baby boy** and press *Enter* or click *Search*. I would also try the following search, to increase the results: **0-3 month baby boy**.

The results will appear, with auctions due to finish soonest at the top of the list (click the *Sort by* button to change this). If there are no matches in Australia, eBay will show you matches from other countries.

Keep an eye along the left hand side of the screen once you've done a search – you can refine the search further using the *Search Options* about halfway down. Search options include:

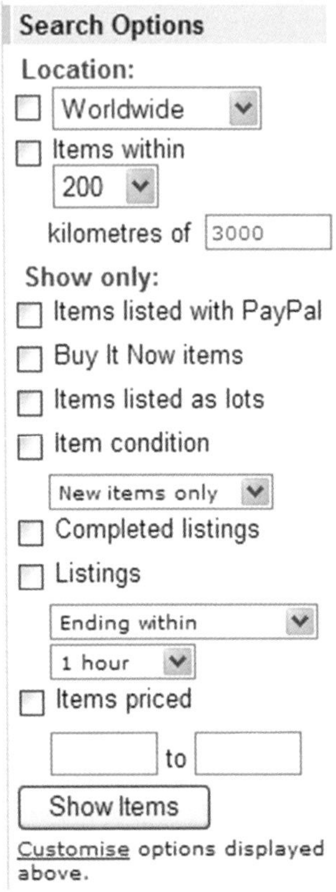

- A location (try *Worldwide* if you're a collector).
- *Buy It Now* items.
- Items listed with PayPal.
- Items ending soon.

You will also notice that listings will have either:

- A small photo alongside the listing (a preview of the photo is included on the main page); or
- A camera icon (which means there is a photo included on the main page); or
- Nothing (which means a photo is not provided).

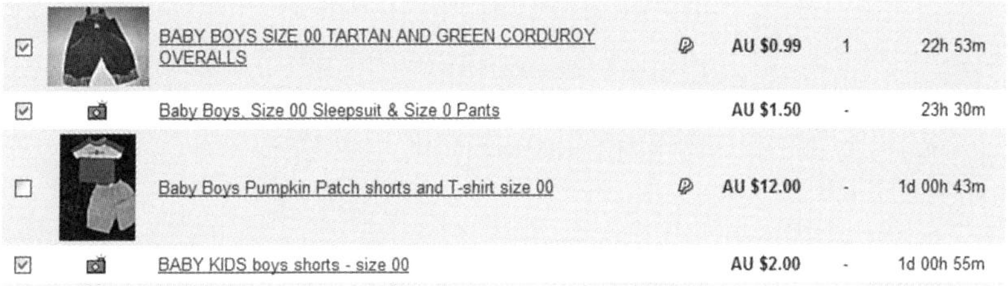

BABY BOYS SIZE 00 TARTAN AND GREEN CORDUROY OVERALLS
AU $0.99
1
22h 53m
Baby Boys, Size 00 Sleepsuit & Size 0 Pants
AU $1.50
-
23h 30m
Baby Boys Pumpkin Patch shorts and T-shirt size 00
AU $12.00
-
1d 00h 43m
BABY KIDS boys shorts - size 00
AU $2.00
-
1d 00h 55m

If there are a number of items you'd like to view, click the checkboxes next to them, then click the *Compare* button.

— Compare Items

Watch All		Remove All

	Remove Item	Remove Item
Item	BABY KIDS boys shorts - size 00	Baby Boys, Size 00 Sleepsuit & Size 0 Pants
	Bid Now! Watch this Item	Bid Now! Watch this Item
Time Left	1 days 0 hours	23 hours 26 mins
Bids	0 bids	0 bids
Seller	lizzieooo (2026 ★) 99.9% Positive	jatsgwobsession (25 ☆) 100% Positive
Price	AU $2.00	AU $1.50
Postage	AU $3.00, Regular	AU $4.50, Regular
Posts From	Australia	Australia
Payment Methods	Bank Deposit EXPRESS Money order/Bank cheque	Other - See Payment Instructions for payment methods accepted

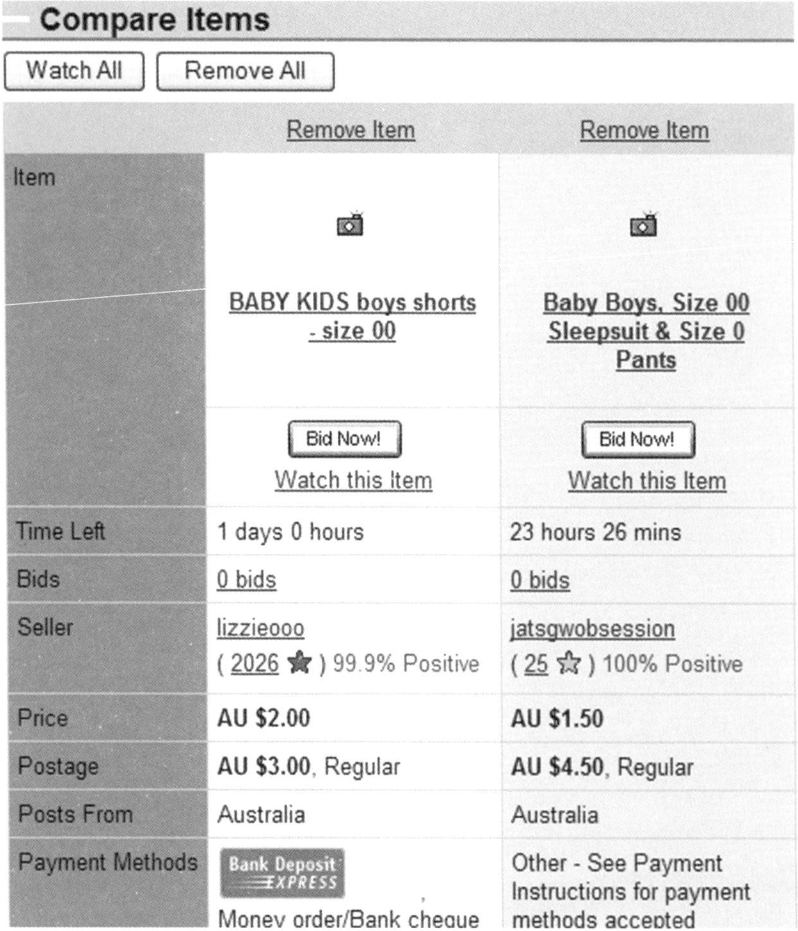

Browse

If you're not sure what you're after or you just want to go 'Windows' shopping, make a cuppa, click the *Buy* button at the top of the eBay home page and you'll be presented with an extensive category listing which you can click through.

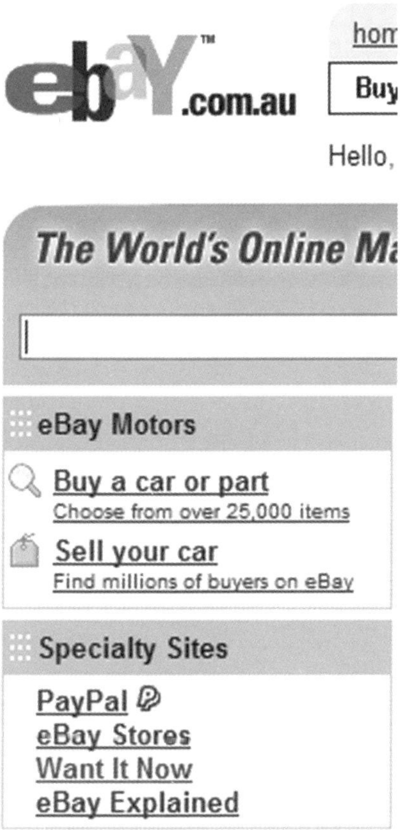

Post a 'Want It' ad

Can't find it on eBay today? Along the left of the eBay homepage under *Specialty Sites* is a link for *Want It Now*, where you can post an ad for an item you're looking for. Sellers often browse these categories and will list an item that matches your ad, then you'll be notified by email although you are not obliged to purchase it.

Find out more

Once you find an item you'd like to keep an eye on, click either the gallery photo or the description to find out every available detail, including:

- Larger photos.
- Auction end date and time.
- Detailed description.
- Bid history.
- Postage cost, payment and returns policies.
- Seller profile and feedback score (see my section on Feedback, page 177).

Click *Ask seller a question* if you'd like more information via email about the item.

Note When buying clothes or shoes, be aware that sizes differ between countries. Check the measurements closely and ask the seller to clarify.

Watching

Unsure whether you want to place a bid on the item, but don't want to lose track of it? Perhaps the auction end date is many days away and you don't want to be the first to bid? Keep an eye on it by clicking *Watch this item* (just above the Seller information). You can use your *My eBay* page to check it out at a glance later.

Bidding

Proxy Bidding

eBay uses a system called proxy bidding, in which you enter your maximum bid (which is kept private) and eBay bids for you in minimum increments up to your maximum amount, keeping you in the highest bid position until your maximum is reached. (Read this again: it makes sense the second time!)

The minimum increment varies depending on the current highest bid of the item. Eg. $1-4.99 = $0.25 increment; $5-24.99 = $0.50 increment, etc.

If the item is listed as an *online auction*, you can make a bid. If you're the first bidder, you'll have to equal the starting bid at least. If you see the *Buy it now* icon, you can choose to purchase the item now and the auction ends.

- Click *Place Bid* or *Buy it Now.*
- Enter the highest amount you'd be happy to pay for the item (your maximum bid). Follow the instructions about the minimum increment.

Click *Continue*.

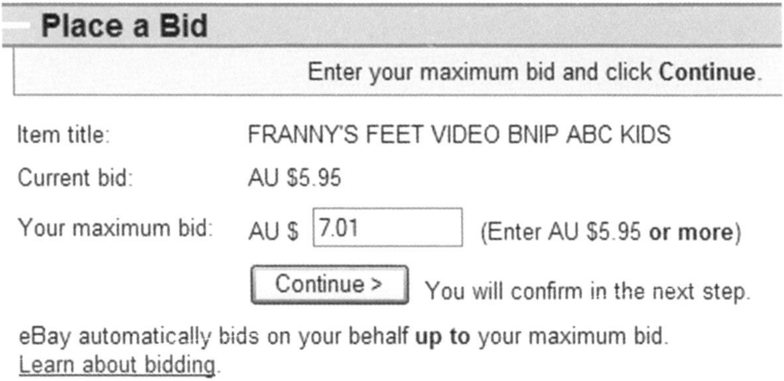

Learn about bidding.

Check the details on the confirmation screen and click *Confirm Bid*.

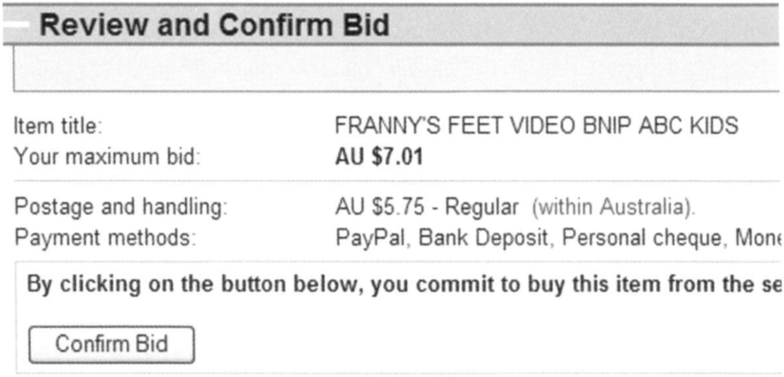

Review and Confirm Bid
Item title:
FRANNY'S FEET VIDEO BNIP ABC KIDS
Your maximum bid:
AU $7.01
(Enter AU $5.95 or more)
You will confirm in the next step.
Postage and handling:
AU $5.75 - Regular (within Australia).
Payment methods:
PayPal, Bank Deposit, Personal cheque,
By clicking on the button below, you commit to buy this item from the
Confirm Bid

The next screen confirms whether you're the highest bidder, and if not, you can choose to make another bid.

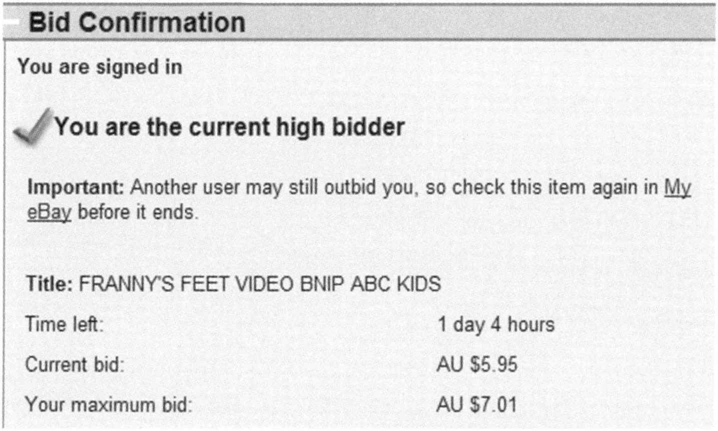

Bid Confirmation

You are signed in

You are the current high bidder

Important: Another user may still outbid you, so check this item again in My eBay before it ends.

Title: FRANNY'S FEET VIDEO BNIP ABC KIDS

Time left:	1 day 4 hours
Current bid:	AU $5.95
Your maximum bid:	AU $7.01

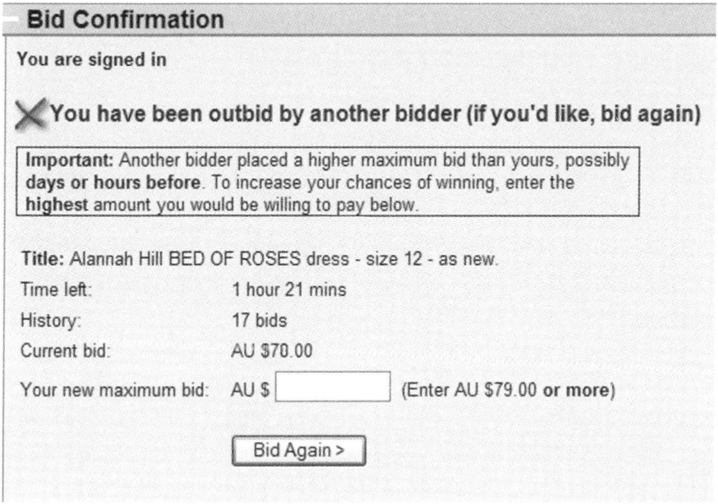

Bid Confirmation

You are signed in

You have been outbid by another bidder (if you'd like, bid again)

Important: Another bidder placed a higher maximum bid than yours, possibly **days or hours before**. To increase your chances of winning, enter the **highest** amount you would be willing to pay below.

Title: Alannah Hill BED OF ROSES dress - size 12 - as new.

Time left:	1 hour 21 mins
History:	17 bids
Current bid:	AU $70.00
Your new maximum bid:	AU $ (Enter AU $79.00 **or more**)

Bid Again >

- Been Outbid later?

If the bidding eventually bypasses your maximum bid, you've been outbid. You'll receive an email letting you know and if you're willing to pay more for the item, place another maximum bid by clicking where instructed.

Backing out of a bid

Placing a bid obligates you to purchase the item if you are the highest bidder at the time the auction closes. There are a few circumstances in which you can retract your bid (but only within 12 hours of the auction closing time):

- The item description has changed significantly since you made your bid.
- The seller cannot be contacted.
- Your bid was a typo (eg: $890 instead of $8.90). In this case, you can retract your bid, but you are expected to place the correct bid immediately.

Make sure you carefully read the information on the eBay site about bid retractions before making a decision.

Last minute bidding – naughty or nice?

It can be a clever tactic to keep an eye on an auction until the very last few seconds and only then come in with your bid – it's called sniping. Why do it? It avoids a bidding war for the item, which inevitably drives the price higher. Although not pleasant for the other bidders, it's not against the rules. To avoid snipers on an item you're bidding on, make sure your bid is the highest you'd pay for the item and eBay will keep bidding for you until the item reaches that price (see Proxy Bidding above).

eSnipe

There's even a separate website, unattached to eBay, called **www.esnipe.com**. You register on eSnipe with your eBay details, then enter an eBay item number you'd like to 'snipe' and a maximum bid. eSnipe will log in to eBay on your behalf a few seconds before the auction finishes and bid up to your maximum amount.

With eSnipe, you can also create a bid group. Say you have $20 to buy a DVD and there are 7 you're interested in on eBay. You can only afford one. On eBay, any bids you place on the items are binding, so you can't bid on more than one. With eSnipe, you put the items into a bid group and as soon as you win one, the other bids are automatically cancelled.

Note If you change your eBay password, don't forget to change your eSnipe password or eSnipe won't be able to bid for you.

eSnipe charges 1% of auctions you win with a minimum of US$0.25 and a maximum of US$10. There is no charge for auctions you don't win. You pay the fees using BidPoints, which you purchase in advance from eSnipe. One BidPoint = US1c, so you'd buy 500 points for US$5.00

Buy it now

Sellers who would be happy with a certain price will add the *Buy it now* option to their listings, allowing you (the buyer) to stop the whole auction process and purchase the item instantly.

Buy It Now

HOT TIP

Make sure you check the postage cost and policies at the bottom of the item window and take them into account.

Paying

When you win an auction, you'll receive an invoice from the seller via email with instructions on how to pay. You can also view the item page on the eBay site once the auction is over.

Common payment methods

- Paypal – use your PayPal account to pay immediately without divulging your credit card details.
- Bank deposit – ask the seller for their bank account details and directly deposit to their account.
- Bank deposit express – some sellers provide their bank account details with their listing, so you can view them as soon as the auction is over.
- Escrow – for large purchases, consider using an Escrow service like the one offered by **escrowaustralia.com.au**. They act as a 'middle man', holding your funds for an accepted 'inspection period' then releasing them to the seller.

Go to the *Help* screens on the eBay site for further info on payment methods.

If the seller offers a *Pay Now* button, click it to have all payment details automatically calculated (handling, postage, insurance, GST, etc).

If you're not sure of the final price, use the *Request Total* button to send an email to the seller asking for it. They will email you back with an invoice.

If you're worried about not receiving the item, choose to pay extra for Insurance, which requires the seller send the item registered mail which means you'll have to sign for it on delivery.

As soon as the seller has received your payment, they are obliged to send the item unless otherwise stated in their payment terms (eg: 'We post items twice a week, Tuesday and Friday').

Shipping

Check the details carefully. Some sellers will charge more than actual shipping costs, eg: some impose a handling and packaging fee. Some overseas sellers don't use regular post but rather a freight service, which can be costly.

Leave Feedback

As soon as you've received your item, leave feedback for the seller.

- Go to your *My eBay* page.
- Use the *My eBay Views* toolbar along the left of the screen, scroll down and click on *Feedback* under the *My Account* heading.
- If you have more than one item to leave feedback for, make use of the *Leave Feedback* button at the top of the list, otherwise click the *Leave Feedback* link alongside the item.

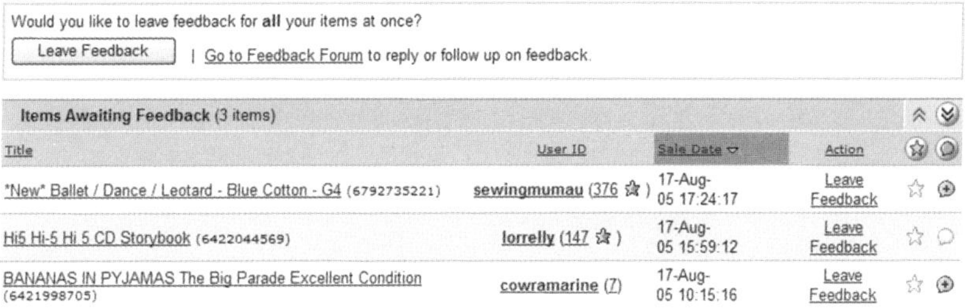

Selling

Create a Seller's Account

Before you can sell anything, you need to confirm your identity by creating a seller's account. You can choose to use either your credit card, a telephone call or snail mail (post). To start selling immediately, go for the credit card option.

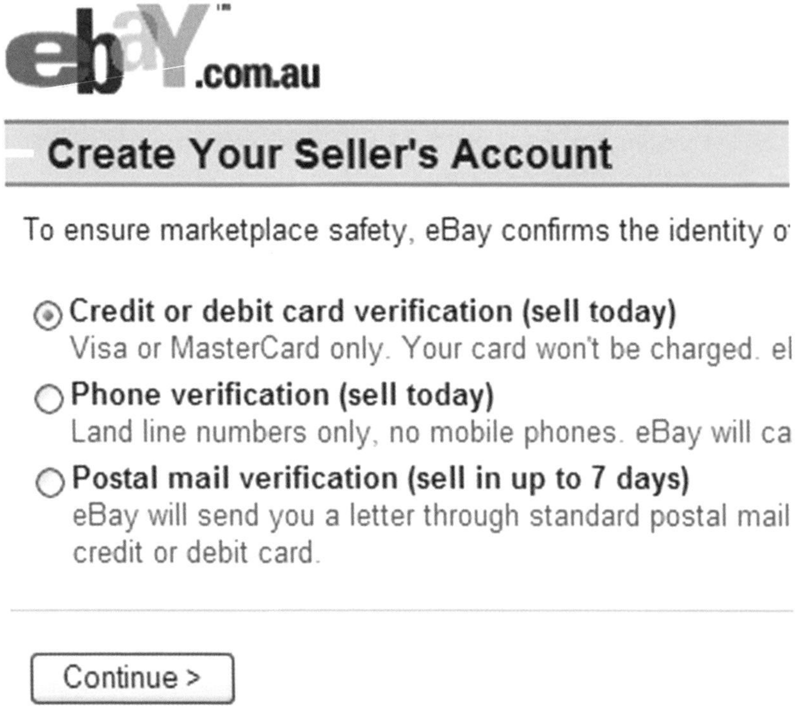
ebay.com.au
Create Your Seller's Account
To ensure marketplace safety, eBay confirms the identity o
Credit or debit card verification (sell today)
Visa or MasterCard only. Your card won't be charged. el
Phone verification (sell today)
Land line numbers only, no mobile phones. eBay will ca
Postal mail verification (sell in up to 7 days)
eBay will send you a letter through standard postal mail
credit or debit card.
Continue >

You can then use this credit card when listing and selling items to have your fees debited.

Get your photos/images ready

Take good digital photos or get scans of your item. I wouldn't even consider listing things without at least one photo – it's free to add the first one (about $0.15 for each additional photo). It is said that photos can increase bids by around 70% and the final price by more than 50%.

Do your research!

Check current listings

Search for items similar to the one you're selling and watch the bid history – you'll get an idea of where to set your starting price. You'll also pick up some tips on how to construct your title, subtitle and item description. (Mostly by taking note of what NOT to do!)

Check completed listings

You can often get a great feel for the going price of certain items by searching for Completed Listings before you list your item.

- Click the *Advanced Search* link at the top of any eBay page.
- Enter your keywords and other search options.
- Click the *Completed Listings Only* box.
- Click *Search*.

Auctions that have ended in the past 15 days will be displayed.

List your Item

Step 1 – Select your category

- Click the *Sell* button at the top of the eBay home page.
- Choose *Online Auction*, then click the *Start a New Listing* button.

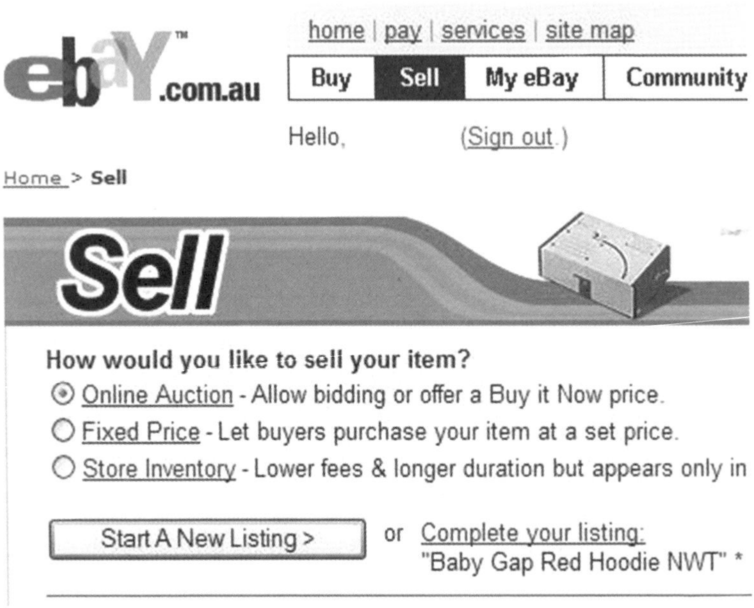

- Browse the category list.

HOT TIP

If you see a red X instead of the Category chooser, you'll need to download an extra Java component which you'll find here:

http://www.java.com/en/download/manual.jsp

- If relevant, list your item in a second category. Sure, you'll pay a second set of fees but you could be exposing your item to twice as many potential buyers.
  eg: If you were selling Auntie Edna's Glomesh handbag, I'd suggest you list it in 'Women's Handbags' as well as 'Vintage Accessories'.
- Click *Continue*.

Step 2 – Describe the item

- Construct an informative title – include the brand, colour, condition and value, always using the accepted abbreviations (see end of this chapter).
  eg: **Baby Gap Red Hoodie 0-3 months NWT (RRP $55)**
- Consider listing a subtitle. Although it costs extra (about $0.50), it is said to increase bids by 74% and increase your final price.
  eg: **Must-have for any funky baby, not available in Aust**
- When creating your Item Description, think about what you'd want to know if you were buying this item. Use the formatting tools available (bold, font size, colour) to make your listing more interesting.

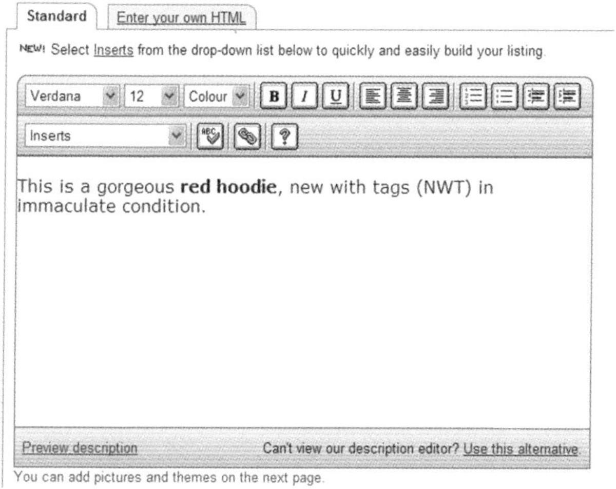

HOT TIP

Cut and paste text from other listings into yours. (See our section on using multiple windows page 162.) If the text is a standard product description from the original packaging or brochure, there's no need to change it, but if it's someone's personal description of their own item, edit the text into your own words. Format the text to suit your style.

Note Many buyers will search by item description – so pack as much info in as you can. DON'T 'keyword spam' by using false words just to attract hits. If it's not genuine Ugg boot brand, don't use those words.

Step 3 – Add a picture, starting price and more details

- Enter a low starting price – the bids will usually push the price up pretty quickly.

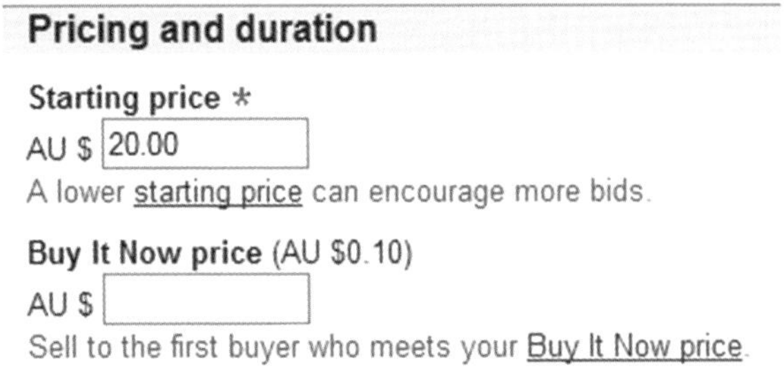

- If you'd be happy to sell your item for a certain amount immediately, enter it in the *Buy It Now* box – that allows a buyer to grab the item at that price without waiting for the auction to finish.

Note You need to have a feedback score of 5 before you can use *Buy it Now* for your listing.

- If the item has real value or is of sentimental value, consider setting a Reserve price.

- The first photo is free but you should consider paying the small extra amount (about $0.25) to add more, especially if your item warrants it – eg: a piece of furniture with a small stain on the back may need extra photos to show all the angles.
- Keep an eye on the tips and tricks provided along the way – read all of the text on each page. It's the quickest way to learn.

Special features

- Use the *Gallery* option (about $0.35) – this shows a small version of your main photo with your listing when it appears in the search results, once a shopper has done a search. As an eBay shopper, I find I'm more likely to click through to an item if the photo is shown in the search results.
- Consider using a design template in the *Listing Designer* section to make your listing more interesting (about $0.10).
- There are other extras you can choose to try and make your listing stand out like *bold*, *highlight* and *border*.
- Add a page counter if you want to be able to see how many people have looked at your listing.

Step 4 – Payment, Insurance and Postage

- When deciding on a payment method, always ensure you've chosen *Bank Deposit* or *PayPal* (or both!) so you'll be paid more quickly.
- Consider offering free postage – it's an extremely popular 'value add' for your item. Think about it – you're getting $25 for a DVD that was just lying around the house, you can cope with $3.80 postage! In this case, you should still add a *Postage service*, but make the amount $0. That way, buyers will know there is no extra charge at the end of the auction.

- When sending valuable items where the buyer has chosen not to pay for registered mail, consider paying for it yourself. It wouldn't be a pleasant situation if the buyer contacted you to say the item never arrived.
- Enter as much information as possible in the *Payment Instructions*, such as a note letting your buyer know there will be no postage added.

Step 5 – Review and confirm

Take your time on the review page, clicking to see a *Preview* of your listing and changing anything relevant by clicking the *Edit* links along the right side of the screen.

When you're certain everything is right, scroll to the bottom, check the insertion fee meets your expectations and, if so, click *Submit Listing*.

GST

It is important to consider your GST obligations. Are you operating as an enterprise? An enterprise covers commercial activities but does not include hobbies. Does your annual turnover exceed $50,000?

YES: You should be registered for GST and include the GST component in your eBay listings.

NO: You don't need to register for or include GST in your listings.

Receiving payment and sending the item

You will receive an email from eBay with your buyer's contact information, including delivery address.

eBay also sends the buyer an email containing your preferred payment methods, adding postage costs if you provided them, and a final price.

Once your buyer has paid, be sure to send the item promptly. Buyers expect items to arrive within 3-5 days of their payment being received.

Second chance offer

If you have more of the same item to sell or the transaction falls through for some reason (ie: you can't contact the buyer or they take an unreasonable amount of time to pay for the item), you can make a Second Chance offer to any of the other bidders.

- Go to your *My eBay* page
- Under the *Items I've Sold* heading, click the *Second Chance Offer* link.

Keep your customers coming back

Ask your buyers via email if they'd like to be notified when you have similar items for sale. Of course, give them the choice to opt out and go off the list if they request it. And be sure to use the BCC field (see our section on Email) to protect your buyers' email addresses from each other.

Ebay terminology

Feedback

The beauty of eBay lies in the Feedback – it's a forum for buyers and sellers to leave feedback about each other for every transaction. The more positive feedback a seller has, the more confidence a buyer has.

When you leave feedback, you'll be asked to choose one of the following and leave a comment:

- Positive = 1 point.
- Negative = -1 point.
- Neutral = 0 points.

You can check any eBay member's Feedback profile by clicking the number next to their name.

You might also notice a coloured star alongside the feedback score – hover your mouse cursor over it to find out what it signifies (yellow = 10-49 points, blue = 50-99 points, and so on).

It is best to leave feedback once the transaction is totally complete – ie: the item is paid for and has been received. It is tempting as a seller to leave feedback as soon as the item is paid for, but I suggest waiting for the buyer to confirm they've received it and are happy.

Leaving Negative Feedback

Don't do it! If you're inclined to leave negative feedback for someone (even if they really deserve it), they're likely to do the same to you. Although you do have the option of adding a response to negative feedback you've received, it really is horrible to lose your 100% positive rating. Leave neutral feedback and a comment that allows others to read between the lines. Or don't leave feedback at all. I know a seller who received a negative feedback rating for selling supposed non-genuine goods, but the goods were perfectly authentic – there goes her perfect record.

Buyer/Seller Relations

Communication is the key! If you have a crisis and can't pay for your purchase until next Tuesday, rather than the Friday you promised, be sure to let the Seller know. And conversely, if you come down with the chicken pox and delay shipping an item by a week, let your buyer know! Respect a potentially very rewarding and social relationship. Don't take it for granted.

Common Acronyms

NBW Never Been Worn

NIB New in Box

NIP New in Packet

MIB	Mint in Box
NWT	New With Tags
NWOT	New Without Tags
BNWT	Brand New with Tags
FS	Factory Sealed

Disputes

No-one wants to invite negative feedback into their profile. In all instances, you should give the other party the benefit of the doubt, at least at first.

Paid for an item and it hasn't arrived? The seller may be caught in a flood-ravaged small town and can't get to the post office!

Sold an item and it hasn't been paid for? The buyer might have computer troubles and is desperately awaiting a call from the fix-it guy!

It is commonly accepted that (unless otherwise listed in the item description) contact should take place between both parties within three days of a completed auction and payment should take place within five days of that. Items should be sent within three days of payment being received.

You should always wait for those times to pass, then try at least one or two extra email reminders before getting worried. If you're a seller, relist the item or send a Second Chance offer to any of the non-winning bidders by clicking the *Second Chance Offer* link on your *My eBay* page.

If you're a buyer and you're not getting satisfaction from the seller about a non-delivered item, you have no choice but to leave negative feedback. The seller is likely to respond that you should have taken out insurance but at least you're warning others. If the same thing happens to other buyers, this seller will start to get a bad reputation.

Always check the eBay website for help on resolving disputes. There is a whole section on *Item Not Received or Significantly Not as Described* and for major disputes you can even pay for online mediation.

Beware!

You may receive emails that look like they come from PayPal or eBay asking you to click and update or confirm sensitive account information, often suggesting that your account may be suspended if you don't follow the instructions. Known as spoof or phishing emails, they are a fraudulent attempt to access your account details, so please delete and ignore them.

PayPal and eBay will never send you an email asking you to enter or confirm sensitive information, so don't be fooled. If in doubt, check the links below.

eBay spoof tutorial: **pages.ebay.com.au/education/spooftutorial/**

PayPal buyer protection info: **www.paypal.com.au** – click on *PayPal buyer protection* along the right.

Note You may also receive fraudulent emails that look like they come from major Australian banks asking for your personal details. All of the banks' homepages have further information about protecting yourself.

Email (using Outlook)

The 90s were revolutionised by the introduction and spread of email. Email has become more and more accessible and has become one of the main reasons we get ourselves connected to the Internet.

It doesn't take long before our Inboxes are full to the scroll-bars with various types of emails – wanted and unwanted. We don't have the access to computer training that we'd like, so we teach ourselves, and often this turns out to be the long way.

Thankfully, there are some good habits, shortcuts and tricks that will speed up your visit to the virtual letterbox.

Although email is the main part of Microsoft Outlook, the full version does include some extremely handy 'productivity tools' like a Calendar, Contact List, Task List and Notes section.

This section assumes you're using Outlook 2000 or above, not Outlook Express, although most things will be identical. Where things are different for Outlook Express, I've endeavoured to mention it.

Outlook shortcuts

Ctrl + N, if you're in the calendar, inbox, contact list, etc.	Creates a new item – either an appointment, email or contact etc.
Ctrl + Enter	Shortcut for Send – useful when you've just finished typing a new email.
Ctrl + Shift + I	Takes you to the Inbox.
Ctrl + Shift + M	Creates a new email message no matter where you are in Outlook.
F5 (or *F9* for Outlook 2003)	Checks for new mail.

Contacts

Contacts do for Outlook what mortar does for a brick house. They are the foundation of the rest of the program. Spend some time setting up your Contacts and you'll find you'll soon be zipping around Outlook like a pro. You can use your contacts to instantly create meetings, emails, assign tasks and visit web pages.

- To quickly create a contact from an email, drag the email from your Inbox onto the *Contacts* folder. A new contact is created with the full name and email address instantly added from the email you dragged.
- *Ctrl* + *N* to create a contact from scratch.
- To quickly create an email from a contact, just drag the contact onto the Inbox. A new email window appears with the email address filled out.
- To email multiple contacts, select them from your contact list by using the techniques already learnt for selecting multiple items, then drag any one of the selected contacts onto the Inbox.
- To create an appointment from a contact ... you guessed it! Drag the contact onto the *Calendar*.
- Use the *View* menu to discover new ways to view your contact list. Address Card view is the most popular.
- Right-click on any contact to see all the different ways you can use it.

Assigning categories to contacts

Assigning a Category to your contacts makes it easier to view them in groups later.

- When creating a new contact, click the *Categories* button at the bottom.

- Click in the box for the relevant category, or to create a new category, click the *Master Category List* button.

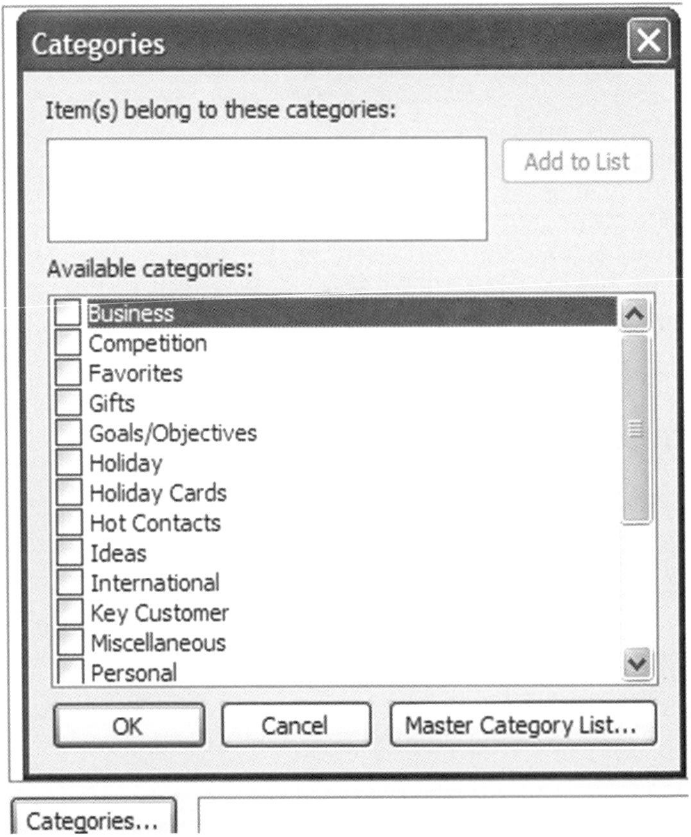

- Click *OK* to finish.

To assign an existing contact (or group of selected contacts) to a category, right-click and select *Categories* from the shortcut menu, select the category and click *OK*.

Viewing Contacts

- Ensure the *Advanced* toolbar is on by right-clicking any existing toolbar and choosing *Advanced* from the shortcut menu.
- Click the down arrow on the *Current View* box (the last function on the *Advanced* toolbar) to view your *Contacts By Categories*. (Remember to use the *plus* and *minus* buttons for each Category heading to show or hide detail.)

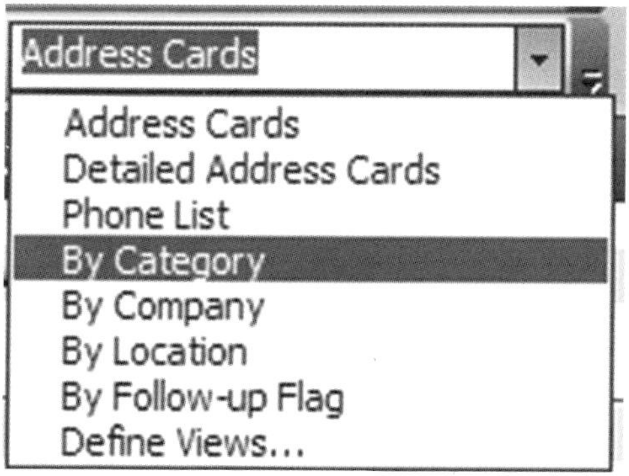

- The most common view is *Address Cards*, in case you want to go back.

Email (the Inbox)

Processing email

I often come across Inboxes that are full of over 200 messages. I tell people they should think of it like their own desk. If you had 200 pieces of paper on the desk, how on earth would you find the one you need? The Inbox should be treated just like the one on your desk at work – it should only contain items that you have yet to deal with. Think of it as your 'to do' list. Check each piece of paper (email), then decide whether to:

Piece of paper	Email
File it in the filing cabinet.	Put it in an email folder.
Throw it out.	Delete it.
Send it to someone else.	Forward it.
Deal with it later.	Keep it in the Inbox.

Creating folders

Once you've read an email and decided that you need to keep it for reference later, but you don't need to action it, you should file it. A well-organised Inbox is the sign of a sick mind, as they say! Well, be sick! Create folders that help you to group emails of a similar subject together – they'll be much easier to find later.

- Click on the Inbox.
- Go to the *File* menu and select *New*, then *Folder*. Notice the shortcut is *Ctrl + Shift + E*, which you can use next time.

  Tip You can also right-click on the Inbox to bring up the shortcut menu to create a new folder.

- Give your new folder a name and make sure that the box below (*Select where to place the folder*) shows it will be appearing in the Inbox.

- Notice that you can use this *Create New Folder* function to create new folders for various Outlook items, such as contacts, mail items and calendar items (Outlook Express does not have these extra functions).
- Repeat for the number of folders you'll need. Take a look at the emails in your Inbox that should be filed, and decide on names for your folders based on those. You can create folders as you're processing your email later, too.

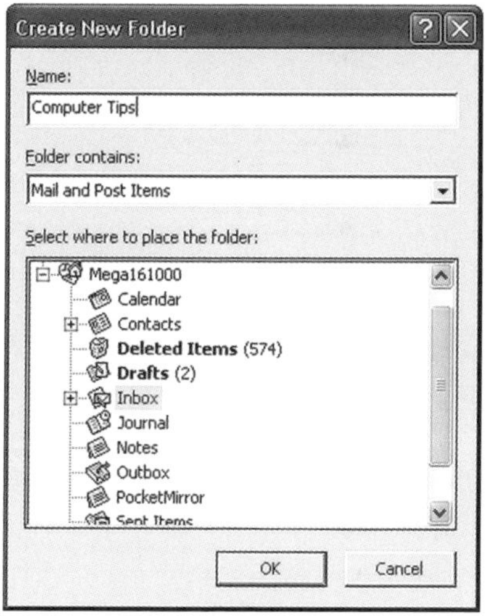

Delete or Rename a folder by right-clicking it and choosing the relevant command from the shortcut menu.

Using folders

Now that you can create new folders, let's move some of those emails out of your Inbox and out of sight!

For Outlook Express:

1 When you're finished reading an email, before closing it, go to the *File* menu and select *Move to Folder*.

Go to step 2, below.

For Outlook Full Version:

1 When you're finished reading an email, before closing it, click the *Move to Folder* icon or go to the *File* menu and select *Move to Folder*. There is also a shortcut – *Ctrl + Shift + V*.

2 Select the folder for the email and click *OK*.

3 Continue for other messages you wish to move.

You can also drag emails from the Inbox into folders you've created by simply clicking and holding the left mouse button on the email, dragging to the new folder and letting go.

Selecting a group of emails

There will be times, especially if you decide to clean up an overloaded Inbox, when you'll want to select more than one message at a time to delete or file. You can either select a block of them or a group at random.

To select a block:

1 Click on the first email once to select it.

2 Move the cursor (no clicking!) to the last email – using your scroll bar if it is off the screen.

3 Hold down the *Shift* key and click once on the last email in the block.

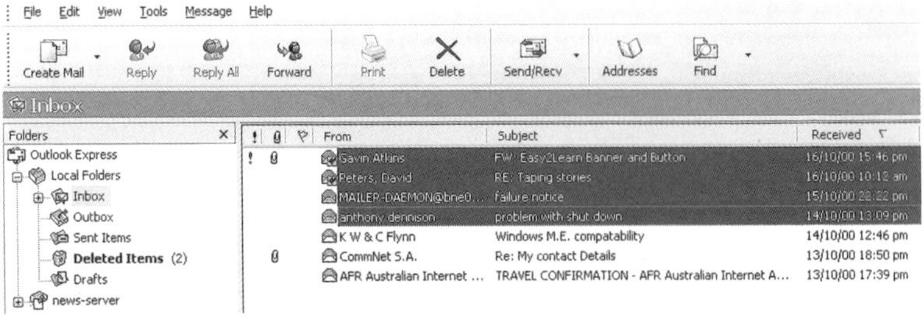

To select multiple emails randomly:

1 Click on the first email once to select it.

2 Move the cursor (no clicking!) to the next email – using your scroll bar if it is off the screen.

3 Hold down the *Ctrl* key and click once.

4 Repeat step 3, above, for all emails you want to select.

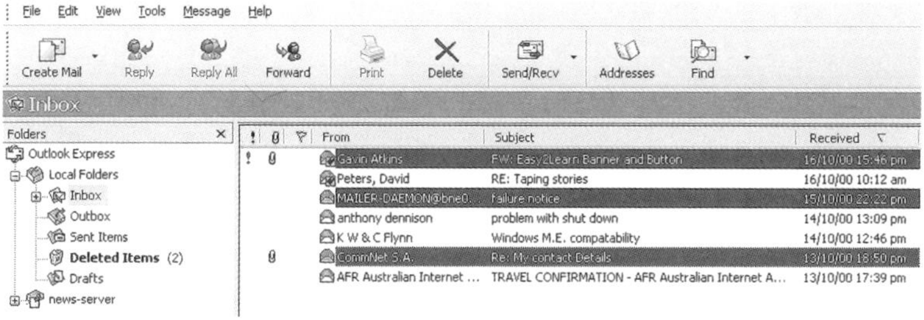

To get rid of the selected emails, either press *Delete* on your keyboard or move them to one of your new folders using the techniques you learnt in 'Using folders' (see pages 195–96).

Attachments

Email is a great way to send files from one computer to another. Most people these days will email files between home and work and colleagues and family members. You can send digital photos, scanned items, documents, anything you'll find on your computer.

Attaching photos to email

Outlook and Outlook Express

When composing a message, click the little paperclip icon on the toolbar or go to the *Insert* menu and select *File*.

After you've clicked the paper clip icon and attached your photo, you can click the *Attachment Options* button to have some control over how the image is sent.

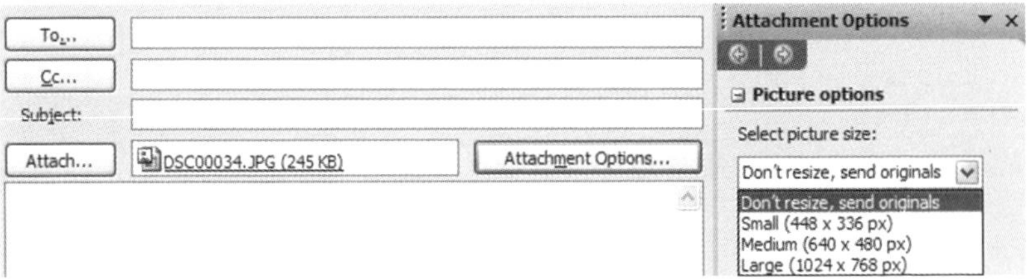

- Once you've clicked the *Attachment Options* button, the Task Pane appears. At the bottom, change the *Select picture size* setting to suit. Mostly, the small size will be fine.

If you choose your pictures from Windows Explorer (before you even get into Outlook), and use the shortcut menu to send them as email attachments, Windows will ask you if you'd like to resize them.

- *Windows key + E* to get to Windows Explorer.
- Navigate through the folders and find your image(s). Usually in the *My Pictures* folder.
- Hold down the *Ctrl* key and select multiple images, or just click the one image you'd like to send.
- Right-click on any of the selected images and from the shortcut menu, choose *Send To, Mail Recipient*.

- Windows asks you if you'd like to resize the pictures to make them easier to send and view. Click *OK*.

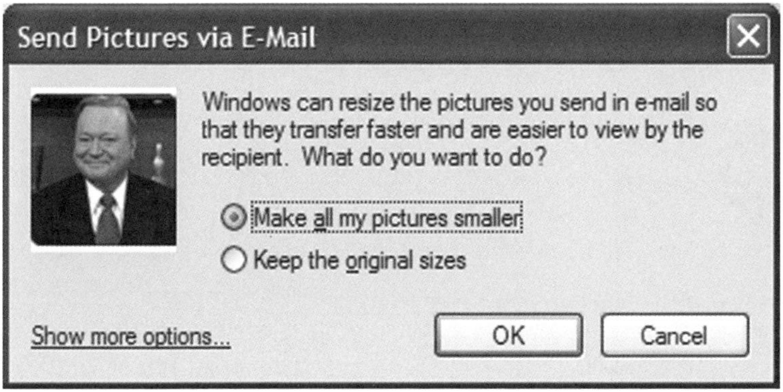

Hotmail

- When composing a message, click the *Add/Edit Attachments* button.
- Click *Browse* to find the file on your computer.
- Click *Attach* to move it to the *Attachments* box.
- Click *OK* to get back to your email.

Sorting Email

- Click on any of the headings at the top of your email list to sort the emails in that order (ie: *Subject, From, Date Received*).

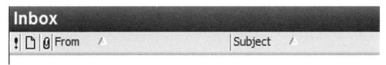

- Click on the same spot again to change to reverse order.

- Hold the *Shift* key down to select a second sort criteria. eg: Click once on the *From* field to sort by sender, hold the *Shift* key down and click on *Subject* to sort by sender followed by subject.

HOT TIP

Once sorted in alphabetic order, press any key on your keyboard to jump quickly to the list of emails starting with that letter.

- You can change the subject of any emails in your Inbox, too – just drag over the existing subject and type over it. To edit the body text of an email you've received (Outlook 2003), from the *Edit* menu, choose *Edit Message*.

Finding Lost Email

All is not lost! You can find missing emails by searching on sender's name or even on any text you know to be inside the body text of the email.

- Click on the *Inbox*.
- For a simple search, go to the *Tools* menu and choose *Find* – a toolbar appears above your email list, and you simply type the name or word you'd like to search for, then press *Enter*. Press the *Close* button (*X*) on the right to get back to normal.

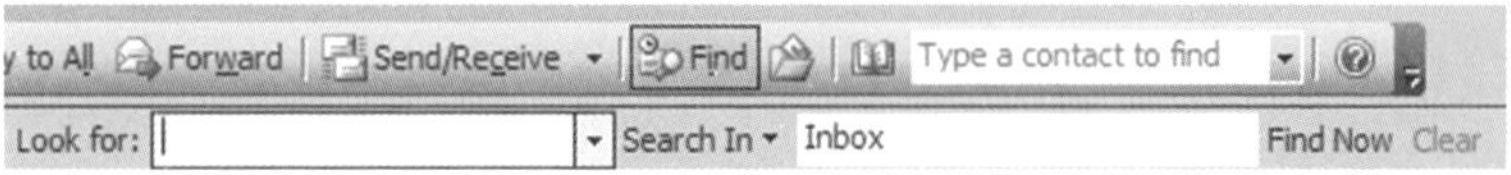

- For a more advanced search, choose *Find* from the *Tools* menu, then *Advanced Find*. Type in your search criteria and press *Enter* to conduct the search. *Close* the Advanced Find window to finish.

Create an Automatic Signature

Your automatic signature appears at the bottom of all newly created emails – it's a great way to save time and look more professional!

- From the *Tools* menu, choose *Options*.
- Along the top, click to select *Mail Format*.
- Click the *Signatures* button at the bottom, then click *New* and give your signature a name.
- Click *Next*, set up your signature and *OK* to finish.

Create an email distribution list

Often sending an email to the same group of people? Create a distribution list, add those people to it, then send the email to the list name instead!

- From the *File* menu, choose *New*, then *Distribution List* or use the shortcut *Ctrl* + *Shift* + *L*.

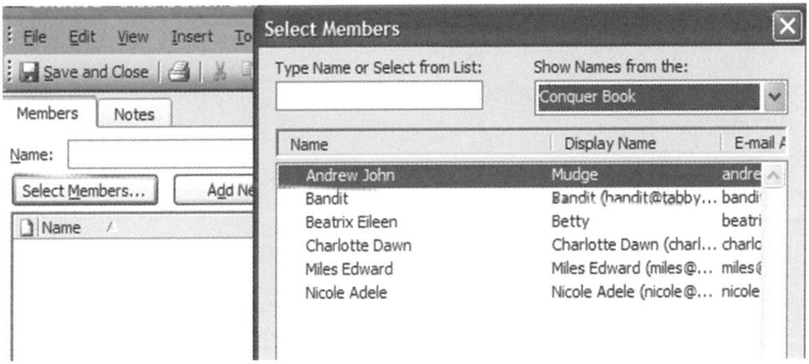

- Give your list a name and click *Select Members*.
- Use the *Ctrl* key to select multiple members and click the *Members* button to add them to the list.
- Click *OK*, then the *Save and Close* button.
- Now, when composing a new message, simply address it to the Distribution List name and everyone in the list will receive it.

Email Quick draw

Here's the slow motion version of the way I create and send an email in a few seconds:

- *Ctrl* + *Shift* + *M* brings up a new email window, no matter where I am in Outlook.
- Type part of the recipient name and Outlook will do the rest, because the name is in my Contact list
- *Tab, Tab* past the CC field and into the Subject field.
- Type a concise subject, *Tab* to the message body which already contains my automatic signature.
- Type a message.
- *Ctrl* + *Enter* is the shortcut for Send.

Junk mail (spam)

Just like your normal letterbox, it is inevitable that you'll start receiving junk mail once you've had your email account for a while.

The best thing to do is ignore emails from strangers and newsletters you have not subscribed to. Replying or attempting to unsubscribe will confirm that your address is valid, and it may even be sold to marketing companies.

Don't be tempted to reply or engage in a conversation with the senders of these emails – even if there is a button, link or invitation to 'be removed from this mailing list'.

It is only safe to unsubscribe from newsletters that you originally subscribed to yourself.

Inbox filtering

You can set up certain Inbox rules that tell your email program how to process your incoming messages. This allows you to delete messages that are inappropriate ('delete messages that contain the word "nudity"') or even send messages to particular folders ('move messages with the word "tennis" to the "sport" folder').

Spending some time creating these rules can be very effective in keeping your Inbox clear of junk, and it is my method of choice, catching about 90 per cent of my junk mail.

Microsoft Outlook Express

- From the *Tools* menu, select *Message Rules* and *Mail*.
- Click to select the *Conditions for your rule*.
- Click to select the *Actions for your rule*.

- Click the blue underlined part of *Rule Description* to define the words you'd like a rule for.
- Name your rule and click *OK*.

Microsoft Outlook

- From the *Tools* menu, choose *Rules and Alerts*.
- Click *New Rule*.
- Follow the instructions, clicking on the relevant rule type in the top window, then clicking the blue *Rule Description* in the bottom window to specify what Outlook needs to look for, and do.
- Click *OK*.

Other Options – K9

Although Australia's ISPs are doing a great job of filtering out rubbish at their level before it reaches us, and the junk mail filters that come with Outlook clean up even more, some ugly email still seems to reach the Inbox, right?

There's an amazing little free tool I found that has been keeping my Inbox clean for a couple of years, and I've had a great response from those I've recommended it to – it's called K9 and comes from a guy called Robin Keir.

The instructions on the site can be quite complex, so I've created a step by step guide to getting it right.

You'll find it on my website at **www.getmega.com/k9**.

Viruses

A virus is a small piece of software code attached to a computer file. Viruses are contagious – they spread from file to file on your computer.

Viruses spread to other computers from disks, emails or the Internet. Once a file with a virus makes it onto your computer, it checks for other files it can attach itself to. Viruses are written by vandals to cause mischief and are attached to files that are likely to be downloaded, sent or copied onto many computers.

Purchasing and installing anti-virus software is necessary, and keeping it up-to-date is essential.

Virus flavours

- 'Malignant' viruses are designed to cause real damage to your files and/or your computer. These are the nasty viruses that do things like add messages to or delete your documents, or even erase your entire hard disk.

- 'Benign' viruses are not designed to cause any harm to your computer or its files. This type of virus is usually designed to be a nuisance.

Macro viruses

Remember the Melissa and Love Bug viruses? These particular viruses use the macro language behind Microsoft Word to spread very quickly – firstly to other files on your computer and then to other computers via files that you email or copy to others. The Melissa virus in particular was spread via email – so if you opened a file that had that virus, it would send itself to the first 50 people in your address book via your own email system.

New Microsoft applications have virus protection features designed to combat macro viruses, which are enabled by default and will bring up a warning if you try to open a document that contains automatically executing macros.

Eek! How to protect yourself

Anti-virus software is an essential purchase. Check out Symantec's Norton Internet Security, PC-cillin, McAfee and Vet.

Virus checking programs will check:

- Disks as you insert them.
- Programs as you execute them.
- Email and Internet files as you download them.

Good ones come with an option to regularly update your program via the Internet or diskette.

There's a free anti-virus program that's been doing the job for me for many months now, and I've put all friends, family and clients onto it. It's called AVG by Grisoft and the robust, reliable free version also updates itself every time you're online.

Get it at **www.free.grisoft.com**. Scroll to the bottom and click the link to download, then scroll to the bottom of the next page and click the installation file.

Email viruses

Most of the time, you can safely open an email and read it without fear of a virus appearing until you open an attachment. However, there are viruses that can find their way to your computer even in emails without attachments. Updating your anti-virus program should protect you from these, but you should also make sure you have installed all the available security updates and patches for your email software (visit the Microsoft site if you are using Outlook or Outlook Express).

Hoax emails

These might come in the form of chain letters or virus warnings.

Chain letters:

An email that sounds just like one of those chain letters you used to receive as a kid is just that – a gimmick. It is not possible that Microsoft will send you $1000 if you send the message to 10 friends. It is not possible that a cure will be found for a child's disease if you send the message to your entire address book.

Phishing or spoofing

Beware of emails that ask for sensitive information such as account login and passwords. This is called 'phishing' or 'spoofing'. The emails seem to be from reputable sources such as your bank, eBay or PayPal, but are, in fact, very clever hoaxes designed to steal your personal information! When you click to enter your details, the site even looks real but you're actually giving your information to a bunch of hacksters!

The banks, eBay and PayPal have all agreed that they will never ask for personal information in an email. They won't even ask you to 'click here' to go to their site and enter the information.

If you receive an email like this, just delete it. If you're concerned about the message in the email – for example, if it's advising you that your account needs updating or it will be suspended – go straight to the site in question manually by typing the address in a new browser window. Do NOT click to it from the email. Login and ask a question using the official methods.

Virus warning hoaxes:

A common hoax going around on email is one that tells you to search your computer for a file called 'jdbgmgr.exe'. The email warns that the file, (which comes with a teddy bear icon), is a virus, and should be deleted. In actual fact, the file is a necessary system file and should be left alone. (If you've already deleted the file, go to **support.microsoft.com** and type the file name into the *Search* box to get instructions on how to put it back.)

The first way to identify a hoax virus warning email is to check whether it mentions that the virus warning has been issued by Microsoft or AOL on their websites. They do not issue virus warnings on their websites.

The emails usually tell you to forward the warning to everyone in your address book. Don't! The best way to be covered for any viruses is to make sure your anti-virus software is up-to-date.

Sometimes it's really hard to work out whether a message is the real deal, so first check a couple of great websites:
www.symantec.com/avcenter/hoax.html
www.us.sophos.com/virusinfo/hoaxes

Etiquette

Email etiquette is as simple and important as the good manners we use every day when dealing with people and in those old days when we used to hand-write letters. Here are the top tips that should prevent you getting in trouble with your email buddies!

- DON'T TYPE IN ALL CAPITALS! When you were reading that, did it sound louder in your head? That's because ALL CAPITALS looks like you're yelling. Save them for when you really want to emphasise something.
- It is extremely difficult to convey emotion using email, and too easy to misinterpret short, sharp points as abrupt. Think carefully about your words and use little emoticons to smile at the end of sentences to help the mood! :-)
- Get to the point. Your reader is much more likely to read your entire email if you're not including superfluous words, sentences and paragraphs! Like the sentence you're reading right now – it's not really necessary is it? ;-)
- If you're replying to an email and it's important that the recipient can refer to their original email, make sure you include it with your reply.
- Similarly, if you're forwarding an email, make sure the recipient understands the entire thread of the conversation by including the original message(s).
- Carbon copy: When sending an email to one person and discussing others, it is good etiquette to include those others on your Cc list.
- Blind carbon copy: If you would like to Cc someone without the other recipients knowing, use the Bcc option.

  Outlook Express: When composing a message, select *View*, *All Headers*, then type the name in the Bcc field.

  Microsoft Outlook: When composing a message, select *View*, *Bcc Field* and type the name in the Bcc field.

HOT TIP

If you want to send a message to a group of people without divulging everyone's email addresses, put them all in the Bcc field and address the message to yourself. That way, the recipients of the message will not see each other's addresses.

- If you're one of the people in a large list of recipients and you'd like to reply, be VERY (See, I used capitals to emphasise a point!) careful when deciding whether to reply to the entire group. You have probably already experienced the annoyance when you're party to a reply that should really be taking place between one person and the original sender.
- If you know someone has a dial-up Internet connection through a standard modem, or they are working from home, check with them before you send large attachments, and especially videos and animations. There is so much junk floating around on email and some people would much prefer not to waste their time on it. It's much less time-consuming (and cheaper if they are paying by the megabyte for downloads) for the recipient if you send a link to a website with the information on it.

Calendar

This is an extremely useful electronic calendar that integrates with the rest of Outlook (not relevant for Outlook Express). You can simply drag a Contact name to the calendar and a new appointment will be created. You can also set reminders to pop up for each appointment and code them according to importance.

You can line up non-consecutive days to compare your schedule:

- Click on the *Calendar* to view it.
- Click on the first day you want to view, then hold down the *Ctrl* key while you click on the other days.

Photos

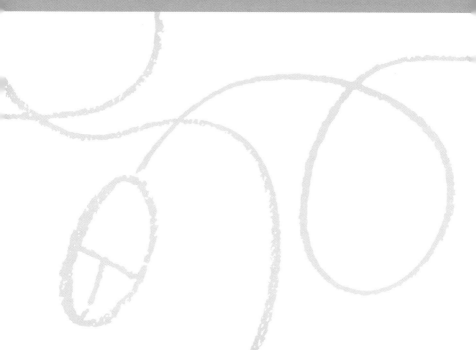

Digital cameras

By now, we have all seen someone in a restaurant or at a party taking pictures and then viewing them immediately on their digital camera, deleting the ones they don't like, laughing at the moments they've captured. It's one step better than Polaroid – we get instant results without the cost of film.

It can be confusing to jump into the world of purchasing a digital camera, but understanding the jargon is the missing puzzle piece.

Megapixels

You will find the capacity of a camera is often referred to in megapixels.

'mega' = 1 million.

The more pixels in your image, the higher the resolution, which means a better quality image. If your snapshots are only to send via email to be viewed on a computer screen, low resolution will be fine. If you want to be able to send your shots to a newspaper or have them used in professional printing, you'll need to go for something with a high resolution.

For the average person, who wants to store and email photos on the PC and print the occasional image, don't settle for less than 3 megapixels.

Of course, the more megapixels, the more expensive the camera!

Zoom type – optical vs digital

- Optical zoom works the same way as a normal camera, by magnifying the image before it is recorded.
- Digital zoom magnifies the image after it is recorded by enlarging the pixels. This gives a lower quality image that can sometimes look grainy.

Storage

Digital cameras do not use film. Instead, they store the images on memory either within the camera, or on memory cards or sticks.

Examples of memory brands include SmartMedia, Sony Memory Stick and CompactFlash. Your camera sales-person and the manual will help you to determine the type of memory you need to buy.

With a 2-megapixel camera, you'll only get about 10 high quality images before you run out of space on an 8Mb memory card. Most people will buy an extra, higher capacity (eg. 128Mb) memory card at the time of purchasing the camera. Turn the photo quality settings down a touch on the camera setup menu – then you can fit hundreds of photos before running out of space!

Of course, there is no need to be concerned about space if you have regular access to a computer into which you can plug your camera and download the stored photos, clearing the memory card for a new batch.

Battery types

Cameras that take normal alkaline batteries are easier to recharge on the road – you just change the batteries. Cameras that come with lithium ion batteries give you much more battery time, but you'll need to take a power pack or recharge unit with you.

With a camera priced in the middle range ($300-500), you should get about 250 good quality photos before running out of battery.

How to choose a digital camera

Okay, now that you understand all of the terminology, how do you choose a digital camera?

There are two questions you need to ask:

- What are you going to use the camera for?
- What is your budget?

Once you have the answers to those two questions, any good digital camera retailer will be able to help you. They'll guide you in choosing the camera that will best suit your requirements within your budget.

Once you've narrowed down the features you'll need in your digital camera, shop around for a good deal. You may find that the prices won't differ greatly, but the extras will – look for a tripod or carry bag or extra tapes. Some camera shops even offer free courses in digital photography.

For good deals online, visit **www.buy-n-shoot.com**

There is a terrific site called **www.shortcourses.com** which gives a complete guide to digital cameras, and where you'll find a section called 'A Short Course in Choosing a Digital Camera' – and it's free!

Digital video cameras

Those of you who'd like to take a further step into the digital image recording world should check out Peter Blasina's Video Camera Magazine website, **www.videocamera.com.au** with tutorials, buying guides and info on video camera clubs.

Scanners

There are many items such as photos, newspaper clippings and children's drawings that you might want to send or store electronically. How do you get them onto the PC? With a scanner of course.

A scanner works just like a photocopier, except it is connected to the PC. Once installed, and with your PC turned on, you place your item face-down onto the scanner, close the lid and usually press a button on the scanner. The scanning software will appear on screen, and you just follow the instructions.

Make sure you choose a scanning type to suit your item: colour photograph, black and white, text, etc.

Make sure you file the item in a location you'll remember. Often people get everything right but they can't find the image they've just scanned!

Emailing photos

Most email programs have a toolbar button with a paperclip icon on it.

When you're composing a message, simply click the paperclip icon and navigate to the file you want to attach to the email message. Double-click it and you're done.

You can also go to the *Insert* menu and select *File*.

Tip Make sure your images are in JPG or GIF format if sending via email. These are the most efficient formats for saving space and allowing most people to view them.

For help attaching photos to email, see the extensive instructions in the Email section, pages 198–99.

Storing and Management

Photos from your digital camera will more than likely be appearing in the *My Pictures* folder on your computer. Some cameras will create their own folder within My Pictures (like 'Kodak'), and then a sub-folder named with the date of the download – like *2005-08-30*.

After a while, it's going to be necessary to find a photo management tool that will help you group your photos into relevant topics, so you can conduct a search based on those topics to quickly find photos such as 'holidays', 'kids', 'grandparents', 'birthdays', etc.

There are some great programs out there, such as Microsoft's Digital Image Suite, that will index your photos and allow you to assign keywords, create innovative slide shows and gift CDs, etc, but I have been really impressed with a free Google tool I found.

picasa.google.com – is there no end to Google's helpful cool tools? The Google browser is like an extra limb for me, and I'm in love with the Google toolbar (see the Internet section), but now I've discovered Picasa, Google's photo management program, I'm cheating on them both. I love Picasa now! Here's how it works:

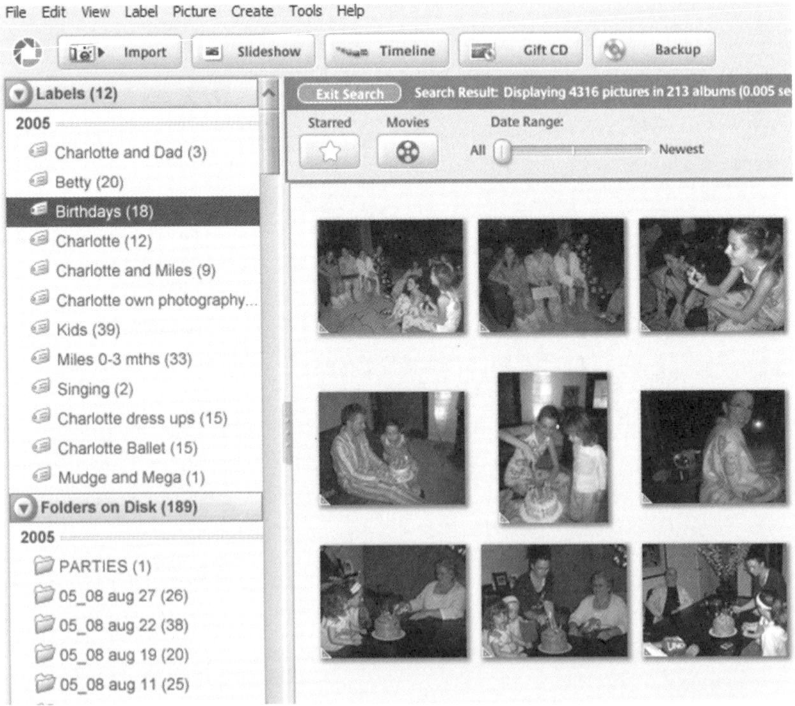

When the program starts, it will find and group all of your photos and videos into collections of folders.

- You can reorganise your pics into the folders you want by clicking and dragging.
- Then, you can spend some time going through and labelling your photos or groups of photos, making it easy to group them or search for certain topics when you need to. Photos can have more than one label.
- In an instant, you can rotate, print, email or even create a collage from a group of photos.

- By double-clicking any photo, you can crop, straighten, fix red-eye and even change the effects to sepia tone or black and white, change the colour saturation and more.

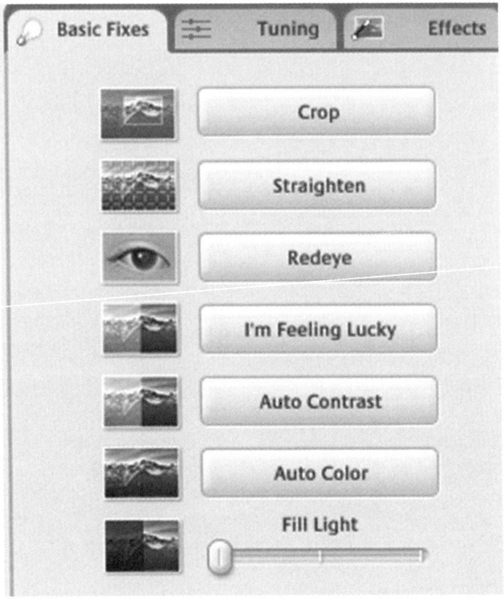

- You can run a slide show of photos, or even create a 'Gift CD'.

Using the Photo Shop or Kiosk

- Have your standard film returned to you on CD at most photo shops these days – just ask when you hand it in.
- Hand your memory stick in to a photo shop anywhere in the world and get them to put the images onto a CD, then clear the memory stick for you.
- Hand your memory stick in at a photo shop and have the images printed as standard photos.

- Use the self service kiosks in large department stores and some photo shops – you insert your memory stick, edit your photo on a touch screen, choose from special borders and decide how many prints you want. Put in your money or credit card and your prints spit out in an instant.

Crafty ideas

The next thing some people want to do, after searching through the Internet and sending emails, is to use their computer to create. Create signs, art, embroidery patterns, T-shirt transfers and even earrings or fridge magnets.

Thanks to some innovative paper manufacturers and printing techniques, it's as easy as the days of Play-doh and Etch A Sketch!

Iron-on t-shirt transfers

Many computer retailers and stationery suppliers sell iron-on T-shirt transfer papers for your inkjet printer. You simply bring up a photo, create an image or message using your PC, and print it out in reverse onto the transfer paper. It is then cut out and ironed onto a T-shirt or other fabric. (You print in reverse, because you've got to place the image face down onto the fabric.)

I've used the Celcast, Hewlett Packard and Kodak papers and they are all great quality, ranging in price from about $16 to $25 for a few sheets.

You'll find instructions inside the pack. Don't worry if your specific printer is not listed in the instructions – it will be a case of trial and error to find the best results for your printer.

- When ironing, follow the paper instructions to the letter. If they suggest an iron without water, comply!
- Iron on a very flat surface.

- Don't create images or words that are too small – do a test print on normal paper and put the paper onto the floor. Stand above it, and if you can make out the image or text properly, it will be big enough to make an impact on a T-shirt.
- Don't forget to print in reverse! I've made that mistake too many times to remember, and it's just a waste of good transfer paper. Do a test print on normal paper just to be sure. Some printers' settings actually have an option to reverse the image automatically. Go to *File*, select *Print* and then *Properties* and you'll find it there under *Mirror Image* or *Reverse*. If your printer settings do not offer this option, you'll need to use a graphics program like Paint Shop Pro to reverse the image.

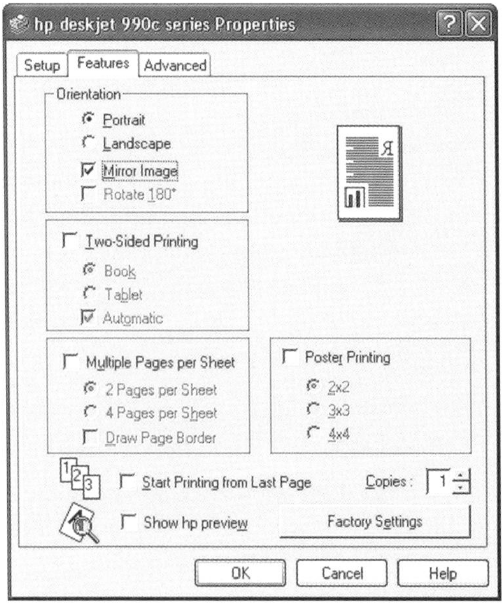

Turn your photos into coffee cups, caps, a bear or photo albums!

Using the web, you can upload your digital photos and have them returned to you in the mail as standard photos/albums or even novelty items like mouse mats, coffee mugs and calendars.

www.bigw.com.au – you download the program first, then use it to choose your photos and products and send the order. You'll have to nominate a store to pick up your order, but most items are cheaper than other online options (photo prints are about 10c cheaper!)

www.fujicolour.com.au – has some interesting options, like putting your photo on a stubby holder ($12.95), baseball cap or teddy bear!

www.myphotofun.com.au – a fantastic new service that will create a gorgeous photo album or calendar from your own photos. First you install the *My Photo Fun Editor*. Then you set up your album, using the supplied backgrounds and layouts and move your own photos around to suit. Then you upload it, pay and await delivery. It's around $25 for the 20-page album, which you can fit almost 200 photos into. It's an awesome gift for relatives. Or yourself!

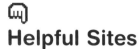

Helpful Sites

The following sites have lots of tips for digital photography – you're sure to find something on each of them:

www.kodak.com.au

cameras.about.com

www.adobe.com/education/digkids/tips

www.nationalgeographic.com/celebrate/tips.html

www.agfaphoto.com.au – click *Support*, then *Photography*, then *Photo Know-how* for the online courses.

www.photographytips.com

What to do when things go wrong

When something happens to your car, you call roadside assistance to get someone to come to you, or take it into your local mechanic. When something happens to your PC, what do you do? You're left searching the net for answers (if it's not your Internet connection that's the problem!), waiting for your computer-savvy friend to call, or wondering how you can convince them to come over again to deal with your temperamental PC. Most people tell me that they just 'muddle through'.

When something goes wrong:

First, take a deep breath.

Second, understand that there are very few things you can do wrong to seriously affect the computer unless you're quite an experienced computer user.

Thirdly, don't take things too seriously. At least you're not the person who called me when I was working on the Microsoft helpdesk to tell me that her computer wasn't working. When I asked her if it was running under Windows, she said 'Oh yes, you've probably got a point there, the guy next to me is under a window and his is working fine!'

Let's go through a few of the things that commonly go wrong that you should be able to sort out yourself, and some 'next steps' if you can't.

Error messages

Getting an error message you don't understand? If it is happening at the same point, such as when you try to open a program or file, or when you try to connect to the Internet, the first thing to think about is what has changed since it last worked correctly? Try uninstalling any new programs, restart and check for the error message and try the installation again.

If the error is related to a printer, scanner or other attached device, check whether it is connected directly to the computer or via another device. If the latter, remove the other devices and attach the troublemaker directly to the computer and see if that solves the problem. You may need to uninstall the device and reinstall (see page 12 and overleaf).

Sometimes cables can be faulty, and I suggest borrowing a friend's matching printer, USB or other cable to see if that solves your problem. If so, you'll need to buy a new cable.

Try the printer, scanner, digital camera or other device on someone else's computer. If the same problem happens, you'll know it's the device itself that is the cause. If it all works okay, your computer may be the issue.

Invalid System Disk

This message is much more simple than it sounds. If you try to start your computer and all you see is a black screen with the white writing 'Invalid System Disk', just replace the disk and press any key to continue. You'll find you've left a floppy disk in the drive, which your computer can't use to start up. Simply eject it and press a key to continue. Thanks to Wim and Feisty for reminding me of this one!

Blue screen of death

The blue screen of death is a term of 'endearment' we have for that screen that takes over your computer sometimes – blue background, white text and very unhelpful! Sometimes the only way to recover from this 'BSOD' is to reboot your computer by holding down *Ctrl* + *Alt* + *Delete*. (See 'Rebooting with the three-finger salute' on page 22.)

Drivers – update them

Drivers are software files that help your computer talk to your hardware device and they sometimes need to be updated, especially if you upgrade your version of Windows.

Go to the website of the manufacturer of your device, e.g. if it is a Hewlett Packard printer, go to **www.hp.com.au** – click *Drivers* and follow the instructions. If it is a Canon digital camera, go to **www.canon.com.au** – click *Support* and then *Download Drivers* and follow the instructions. You will also find many drivers or at least links to them at **www.driverzone.com**

Printer problems

Printers are getting more foolproof with each new model, but understanding some of the common issues may help when you're trying to get that last-minute report, assignment or brochure out.

If you're getting unexpected results and error messages that don't make sense, the first thing to try is to turn the printer off for at least 20 seconds and then back on and try again. Failing that, we'll need to break it down to a few different issues, read on ...

Paper size

Most software, like Word, comes set to a default paper size of US Letter, but our printers expect us to choose A4, because that's the size paper we've put into them. You should change the default paper size to match.

- In Word, go to the *File* menu, then select *Page Setup*.
- Along the top, go to *Paper* and then change the *Paper Size* to A4 (210 mm x 297 mm).
- Don't click *OK* yet – you first need to click the *Default* button to make sure that the change is permanent.
- Click *Yes* when asked if you want the change to affect all new documents.

Messy print

If your printout is missing bits, the culprit is likely to be a clogged cartridge head or nozzle, and luckily this can be fixed – refer to the manual that came with your printer to find out how to clean the cartridge head or nozzle. With most printers, you'll find this option as follows:

- Click on *Start*, *Settings*, *Printers*.
- Right-click on your printer name and select *Properties*.

Installing and uninstalling printers

Whether you've got a new printer or you've tried everything to fix the problems with your existing one, there comes a time when you'll need to uninstall a printer and reinstall the same one or a new one.

To uninstall:

- Click on *Start*, *Settings*, *Printers*.
- Right-click on the printer name and select *Delete*, then *Yes*.

To install:

- Click on *Start*, *Settings*, *Printers*.
- From the *File* menu, select *Add Printer* and follow the instructions.

Cancelling printing

If a long document starts printing and you decide you need to stop it, turning the printer off and back on will not always cancel the print job. You need to:

- Click on *Start*, *Settings*, *Printers*.
- Double-click the Printer name.
- Right-click on the print job and select *Cancel* from the shortcut menu.

Scandisk and Defrag

In the normal working life of a computer, the hard disk is going to take a beating. Even a computer that is only a few months old can have many bits of files all over the hard disk (fragmentation) that can really slow it down. When this happens, you may notice that your computer is making churning or grunting noises. It's a great idea to get into the habit of checking your hard disk and defragmenting it every few months, or even setting the system to do it automatically.

Scandisk

You will notice the Scandisk procedure starts itself up when your computer starts up, if it has been shut down suddenly.

Scandisk checks your hard disk for file corruption or 'bad sectors'. Let it run through every few weeks, but it is safe to exit out of it anytime by pressing the *x* key on your keyboard.

If you haven't seen it pop up at startup for a while and you want to run it:

- Double-click *My Computer*.

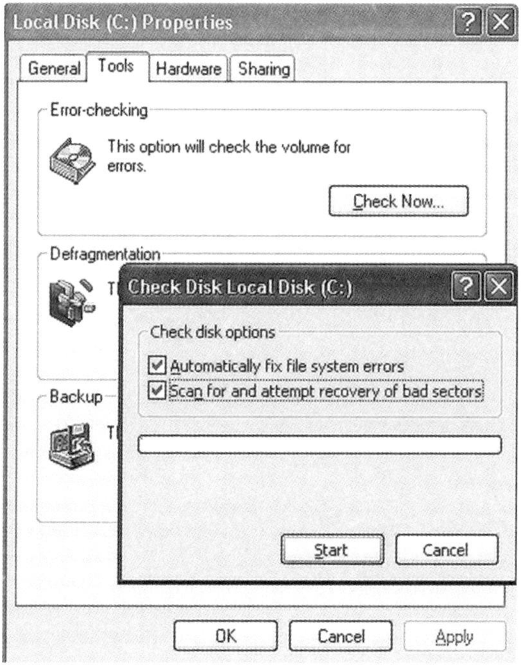

- Right-click the *C: Drive* and select *Properties* from the shortcut menu.
- Along the top, click *Tools*.
- Click *Check Now* and follow the instructions, choosing to automatically repair any errors.

Defrag

Defragmenting the computer can cause it to run more efficiently, as it cleans up all of the little bits of files into blocks.

HOT TIP

Make sure you turn off your screen saver before you do a Defrag because Defrag will restart every time the screen saver kicks in. See the Windows section for instructions on turning off the screen saver.

- Click *Start, Programs, Accessories, System Tools, Disk Defragmenter*.
- Click *Defrag*.

Note This procedure can sometimes take a very long time, and may be best performed overnight.

System information

Whenever you need to find out some technical information about your PC to relay to a more technical person, the System Information tool is the place to start.

- Click *Start* and select *Programs*.
- Select *Accessories* and then *System Tools* and *System Information*.
- The most useful bits of information for anyone technical you're talking to will be in the System Summary:
  - OS Name
  - Version
  - Total Physical Memory

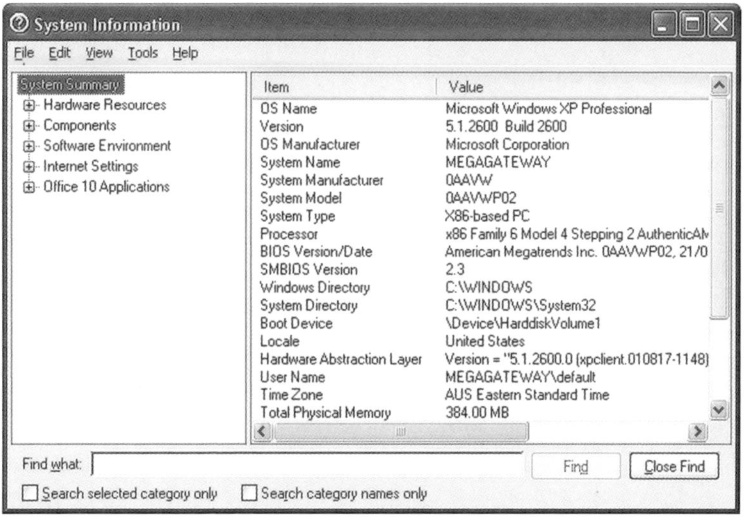

Memory vs hard disk space errors

It is commonly misunderstood that hard disk space and memory are one and the same.

Memory refers to the amount of RAM (random access memory) your computer has. RAM is like short-term memory, holding bits of information in storage while the computer is on, but clearing itself at shutdown. Most computers need a minimum of 64Mb of RAM, but function quicker and more efficiently with more. You will also need more RAM for each upgrade of Windows.

Hard disk space refers to the amount of space you've got on the hard disk inside your computer for long-term storage. The hard disk stores your program files and any documents you create. It also gets cluttered with temporary files that are created behind the scenes by all programs, especially Internet Explorer.

You should often run a Disk Cleanup to get rid of these files, and there's a program that does just that, which comes with Windows. You may also need to run a Disk Cleanup if any error messages appear that suggest you are running low on hard disk space.

- Go to the *Start* menu and select *Programs*.
- Select *Accessories*, then *System Tools*.
- Click *Disk Cleanup*.
- It is safest to go with the default options selected and simply click *OK*.

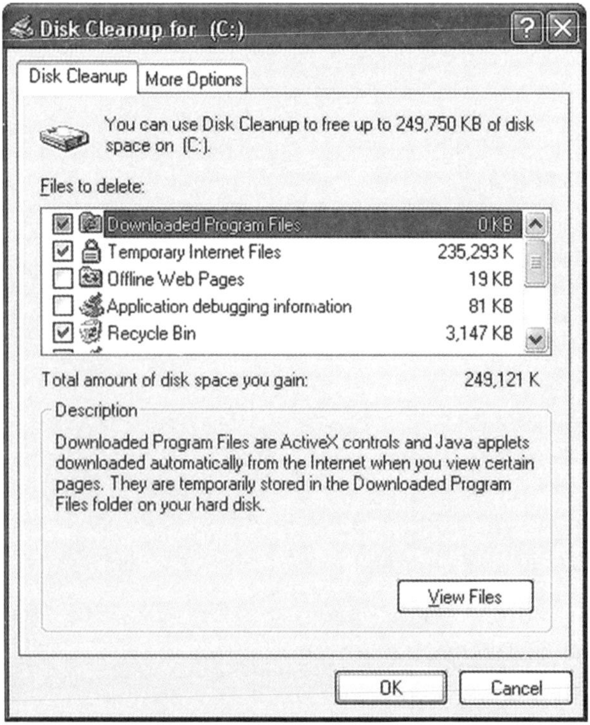

Sound issues

Problems with sound are most commonly related to game play, and can range from scratchy or distorted sound to quiet or even no sound at all. The first thing to check is that your speakers are not muted:

- Double-click the *Speaker* icon in your System Tray in the bottom right corner of Windows.
- Check all of the settings to ensure *Mute* is not selected.

There is an excellent article on the Internet that takes you through all of the sound-related issues you could encounter within Windows, so visit the Microsoft support site at **support.microsoft.com** and type this article number into the Search box: **812394**. Be sure you click the link *Search (Knowledge Base)*, then choose *Article ID* as the Search Type. Article 307918 also has lots of things to try for sound issues.

Device Manager

Sometimes a hardware conflict may happen when your computer has allocated its internal resources to more than one hardware device. You can check for this conflict by following these instructions:

Windows 2000 Professional and Windows XP

- Click *Start* then *Control Panel*.
- Double-click the *System* icon.

- Along the top, click *Hardware*, then *Device Manager*.

- You can double-click any device to find out more about it, then click *Driver* along the top and *Update driver* to try and update the driver automatically.

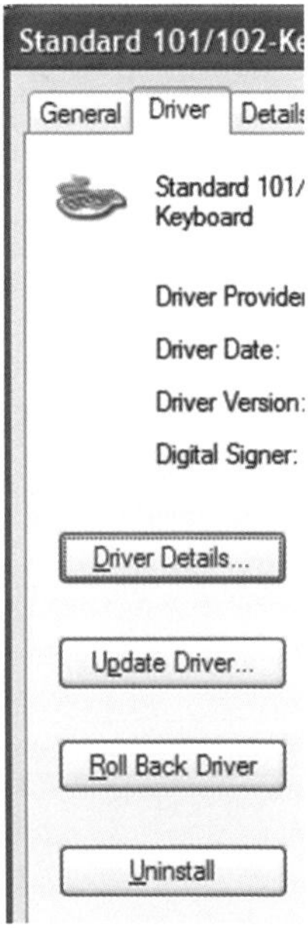

Great web resources for self-help

You don't need me to tell you that the Internet is the place to go when you're trying to find information on just about anything at all. It is probably the most abundant source of information about computers you'll find anywhere, and these sites are some classic examples.

www.microsoft.com – for product information, free downloads of handy additions to products and more.

www.support.microsoft.com – as much as we love to hate Microsoft, they deserve a pat on the back for the amazing online resources available to us all. Here's how to use the support site.

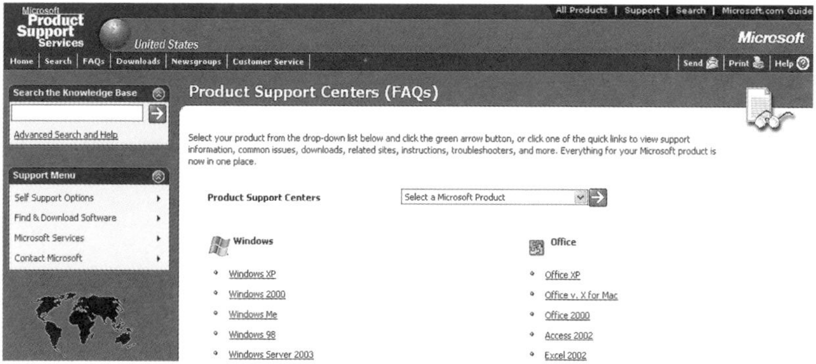

- Click *Search* along the top, and type in the search box, as you would using any search engine, like **www.google.com**. For example, if you're wanting help on mail merge errors in Word, type: **word "mail merge" error**

OR

- Click *FAQs* (frequently asked questions) along the top, then click the product of your choice. For example, click Windows 98 and you'll find a great tool for narrowing down shut-down problems. If you need it straight away, go to **support.microsoft.com/support/windows/tshoot**.

www.driverzone.com and

www.realpchelp.com/drivers.html – a couple of great examples of one-stop shops for drivers of all shapes, sizes and manufacturers.

www.howstuffworks.com – not just computer-related, this site will teach you something new every day.

www.netlingo.com – the best dictionary of Internet terms I have found. It also includes a chat jargon dictionary, to help decipher all of those smiley faces! ;-)

whatis.techtarget.com – a more technical site, but jam-packed with explanations all related to the world of computers.

www.webopedia.com – a combination of the last two sites ... all the definitions you need relating to computers.

Finally, use **www.google.com** to search for sites dedicated to your particular problem, but type the word: **troubleshooting** and you'll be sure to find some help, e.g.: **troubleshooting "digital camera"**.

What next?

www.getmega.com

At the GetMega site, you'll find a wealth of information for computer users of all abilities.

- Visit the free GetMega Helpdesk – a great place full to the scroll-bars with hints, tips, tricks, website reviews and news about Ms Megabyte.
- Visit the GetMega Computer Support Message Boards – a great place to go to ask all of your computer questions and receive friendly help from the GetMega Community.
- Navigate through the site for regular updates on the world of technology, and how it can be used in everyday life.

www.conqueryourcomputer.com.au

The subscription-based online lesson library companion to this book. There are hundreds of mini computer lessons ready to view. You can search any topic, or browse through the contents. When you find a lesson you want to watch, the screen takes over, demonstrating how to get things done, with my voice narrating. You can even print out the instructions for later.

There are a number of sample animations available so you can try before you buy!

Summon a Mega's little helper

Mega's team of friendly helpers are also available to help you in your own home or office. Call 1300 734 904 to book a 2hr session when you're ready. Mention this book and receive $36 off your first booking.

'Safe & Secure' PC Health Check

One of Mega's team will come to you to sweep your computer for net nasties lurking behind the scenes.

The PC Health Check:

- sorts out Viruses and Spam.
- unclutters your hard drive.
- fixes your Internet home page.
- kills popup ads.
- banishes Spyware.
- recommends a backup strategy to protect your precious files and memories.

Call 1300 734 904 to book.

Heartfelt thanks to ...

{{{Mudge}}} – my missing jigsaw piece, for his continual belief, endless support and general va-va-voom factor. Without you ...

Betty, for the bedtime kiss ceremony; Charlotte, for the laughs and dress ups and Miles, for being my little fighter!

Pip – the original domestic goddess, for being the eBay whiz to whom I owe that chapter.

Fonnie, Feisty, Malcolm and Flip – for leading the universe to conspire.

For writing, editing and proofreading, you must visit www.thefeistyempire.com. For marketing expertise, it's got to be www.prozonemarketing.com.au

The Grandies – Nikki & Terry, Dawn & Charles for the never-ending stream of grandchild-related yeses and for being more than happy to be taken advantage of!

Bert – for your ongoing belief in me, your support and encouragement. You continue to amaze and inspire us all.

Bright Club – my 'peeps'! For being my remote office cubicle mates – the priceless sounding board I can't do without.

The FingerTips subscribers and Helpdesk members for your ongoing support, interest and ideas ... without you, there would be no book!

Index